ST BASIL THE GREAT

On Fasting and Feasts

T0339315

ST VLADIMIR'S SEMINARY PRESS
Popular Patristics Series
Number 50

The Popular Patristics Series published by St Vladimir's Seminary Press provides readable and accurate translations of a wide range of early Christian literature to a wide audience—students of Christian history to lay Christians reading for spiritual benefit. Recognized scholars in their fields provide short but comprehensive and clear introductions to the material. The texts include classics of Christian literature, thematic volumes, collections of homilies, letters on spiritual counsel, and poetical works from a variety of geographical contexts and historical backgrounds. The mission of the series is to mine the riches of the early Church and to make these treasures available to all.

Series Editor
BOGDAN BUCUR

Associate Editor
IGNATIUS GREEN

* * *

Series Editor
1999–2020
JOHN BEHR

ST BASIL THE GREAT

On Fasting
and Feasts

Translated by

SUSAN R. HOLMAN and MARK DELCOGLIANO

Introduction by

SUSAN R. HOLMAN

ST VLADIMIR'S SEMINARY PRESS
YONKERS, NEW YORK
2013

Library of Congress Control Number: 2013947637

ST VLADIMIR'S SEMINARY PRESS
575 Scarsdale Road, Yonkers, NY 10707
1-800-204-2665
www.svspress.com

ISBN 978–088141–480–6
ISSN 1555–5755

PRINTED IN THE UNITED STATES OF AMERICA

For all

who love

to feast

and

long

to

pray

Contents

Introduction

Background

Basil of Caesarea (*c.* 329–379 CE) is best known and widely revered for his role in defending the Christian doctrine of the Trinity, and as the founder of a communal monastic model in the Greek-speaking world of late antiquity. His influence in the Christian East is comparable to that of Benedict of Nursia (founder of Benedictine spirituality) in the West. But Basil did much more than simply promote Christian doctrine and live as a monk. As one of the three "Cappadocian Fathers" (with his brother, Gregory of Nyssa, and his friend, Gregory of Nazianzus), Basil drew on his classical education, family ties, and political influence in a Roman civic order to reflect on the persecutions that had shaped his grandparents in the early 300s. Entering public life soon after the death of the anti-Christian emperor, Julian, Basil spent much of his career as a bishop in dialogue with political leaders to try and make Christian policies and practices powerful and secure for the future. He did this very much by working "within" the system of his day, as an elected and ordained clergyman in a well-established hierarchy. He had opinions about material goods and divestment that some scholars have at times identified with twentieth-century "socialism," but he never made any effort to overturn the fundamental political order in his culture. Like the vast majority of his colleagues and acquaintances, he accepted, for example, slavery, authoritarian leadership, and even, sadly, domestic abuse.

Even his theology was sometimes regarded as a bit wobbly. The Arian controversy of the 320s had tempered by the 360s into multiple party schisms, as thinking Christians continued to debate what language and terms best expressed what they believed to be the true doctrine of the divinity of Jesus Christ and his relationship to God the Father. Basil generally took the position of a theological optimist, encouraging dialogue between his friends in their apparent differences, and convinced that they must surely agree with him in a fundamental "orthodoxy." The debates tended to be inflammatory, and he was at times opposed, if only for choosing the wrong friends. For despite his authoritarian tendencies, Basil had many friends.

His writings also clearly express compassion for the needy and a commitment to fair and honest dealings in public life. His social ethics are best known from the accounts of his local responses to relieve the hunger, poverty, and disease in a famine that struck the region sometime around 368–369 CE. These philanthropic ideals and the activities described in his letters, sermons, and his friends' writings, witness to a man eager to defend what we might today call "entitlements."[1] His texts from the famine years argue for a radical divestment that nonetheless respected inheritance and property ownership, and a social equity within the given civic order. His sister, Macrina, and his brother, Peter, were perhaps the real radicals in the family,[2] but Basil, as far as we can tell, truly practiced the lifelong asceticism that he preached.

For all that makes Basil a gifted but flawed and sinful ordinary human being, he retains a revered spot in Orthodox Christianity today, as one of the "Three Hierarchs," alongside Gregory of Nazianzus and John Chrysostom. Some know him for his *Rule*; others know

[1]For Basil's social action and discussion related to the language of "rights," see Susan R. Holman, *The Hungry are Dying: Beggars and Bishops in Roman Cappadocia*, Oxford Studies in Historical Theology (New York: Oxford University Press, 2001); and especially idem, "Healing the World with Righteousness? The Language of Social Justice in Early Christian Homilies," *Charity and Giving in Monotheistic Religions*, Miriam Frenkel and Yaacov Lev, eds., Studien zur Geschichte und Kultur des islamischen Orients 22 (Berlin and New York: Walter de Gruyter, 2009), 89–110.

[2]Philip Rousseau, "The Pious Household and the Virgin Chorus: Reflections on Gregory of Nyssa's Life of Macrina," *Journal of Early Christian Studies* 13.2 (Summer 2005): 165–86.

him from the liturgy that bears his name; for others what stands out, beyond all else, are his sermons. In this book we offer translations of nine sermons that relate specifically to worship events characterized by the liturgical seasons of fasting and feasts.

Basil may have begun to preach in church around 362, when Eusebius, his bishop in the Cappadocian capital city of Caesarea,[3] ordained him presbyter. In this role, he preached—in the city church and in the surrounding regions—until Eusebius died in 370 and Basil was voted his successor. He continued to preach and travel until his own death nine years later. Stenographers transcribed his sermons from their live delivery. As a result, we sometimes find hints of how the audience behaved and how he was often forced to improvise, sometimes at an awkward moment's notice. Of the sermons we translate in this volume, there are hints of this in the way he describes the congregation in his Easter homily against drunkenness. It is also suggested by the way he cuts short his description of the martyr Julitta to finish the homily he had begun, on thanksgiving, the previous day. His sermon on the martyr Mamas also suggests that he was pressed to preach with very little preparation or knowledge about his subject. Basil seems to improvise from the one known fact—Mamas was a shepherd—to weave his address into a theological warning against neo-Arian teachers.

These improvisations were influenced by the fact that Basil could not always choose his sermon topic. Certain festivals in the church year called for particular homiletic themes or subjects. This was especially true for sermons preached at festival events around Christ's birth, baptism, death and resurrection, and in the annual festival liturgies at martyr shrines that celebrated the victorious and often gruesome death of these Christian heroes and heroines. We know a great deal about the fourth-century liturgical year and this cult of saints in Cappadocia, although there are often variant views on certain dates.[4]

---

[3]Not to be confused with the early fourth-century Church historian.

[4]On the cult of saints in Cappadocia, see Jill Burnett Comings, *Aspects of the*

The sermons translated here do not, in most cases, exist elsewhere in a modern English translation that is readily accessible to most Christian readers.[5] In addition to five sermons associated with Christmas, Epiphany, Lent, and Easter, they include three sermons delivered at the annual commemorative festival of a martyr saint—Julitta, Mamas, and Barlaam—and the initial sermon *On Giving Thanks,* which Basil preached the day before his truncated address on Julitta. The nine sermons are organized here in a sequence that broadly follows the Christian liturgical calendar.[6] Since the translations in this book are designed to be most useful to the ordinary layperson and those who might use them in spiritual reflection and religious education, a brief overview of each homily is given below to help provide a basic summary of their context.

On the Holy Birth of Christ[7]

This sermon draws on exegetical traditions about the infancy narratives and traditions about the Virgin Mary that Basil derived from

Liturgical Year in Cappadocia 324–430 (New York: Peter Lang, 2005), and Vasiliki M. Limberis, *Architects of Piety: The Cappadocian Fathers and the Cult of Martyrs* (New York: Oxford University Press, 2011).

[5]For an exhaustive list of the known English translations of Basil's sermons, see Mark DelCogliano, *St Basil of Caesarea: On Christian Doctrine and Practice,* Popular Patristics Series 47 (Yonkers, NY: St Vladimir's Seminary Press, 2013), 307–8.

[6]With two exceptions: First, in the sermon on Mamas, Basil says he is preaching at the beginning of a new year. According to R. W. Burgess, "New Year's Day" in fourth-century Cappadocia was in early October, and yet Gregory of Nazianzus's *Or.* 44, *On New Sunday,* preached during a similar festival for Mamas in Caesarea, is clearly placed on the Sunday after Easter (see below). Given these variations and the sermon itself, it seemed most logical to place *On the Holy Martyr Mamas* toward the end of this collection, with the other martyrs. Second, the sermon *On the Martyr Barlaam* is placed at the end in part because it is generally regarded as pseudonymous, and because there are at least three very different calendar dates associated with its tradition.

[7]*Homilia in sanctam Christi generationem* (=*Chr.,* also identified as *Hom.* 27). The overview here is based on Mark DelCogliano, "Tradition and Polemic in Basil of Caesarea's Homily on the Theophany," *Vigiliae Christianae* 66 (2012): 30–55.

Origen and from Eusebius of Caesarea. Several leading liturgical scholars argue that this sermon is one of the earliest witnesses to December 25 for the Christmas feast.[8] We do not know the year, but it was preached sometime during Basil's episcopate.

After a preface in which Basil speaks about the incomprehensibility of Christ's eternal birth from the Father, he answers a series of questions about the incarnation, posed by an imaginary interlocutor. Some of his statements, particularly those arguing that Christ's flesh was the same as that of ordinary humanity, seem to be directed against the Christological position of Apollinarius of Laodicea.[9] The final question concerns the "workshop" of the divine economy, with Basil arguing that this was located in the body of the Holy Virgin, citing Matthew 1.18. The remainder of the sermon, except for the exhortatory conclusion, is devoted to providing a commentary on selected verses from Matthew 1.18–2.11. Basil draws from his sources selectively to explain the virgin birth, Mary's relationship with Joseph, and the coming of the magi. The way he uses the traditions from Origen and Eusebius likely suggest that he was positioning himself against some of the divergent views of his theological opponent, Eunomius.

On Baptism[10]

Jean Bernardi and other scholars commonly date Basil's sermon on baptism to January 6, the feast of Epiphany, because a similar

---

[8]Thomas J. Talley, *The Origins of the Liturgical Year* (New York: Pueblo, 1968); *2nd* ed. (Collegeville: Liturgical Press, 1991), 138. See also discussion in Paul F. Bradshaw and Maxwell E. Johnson, *The Origins of Feasts, Fasts and Seasons in Early Christianity* (Collegeville: Liturgical Press, 2011), 149–51 (on Christmas) and 192–3 (on the fourth-century festal cycle in Cappadocia). See Burnett Comings, *Aspects of the Liturgical Year in Cappadocia*, 62–69 for a summary of the scholarly debates about the Cappadocian celebration of December 25.

[9]Andrew Radde-Gallwitz, *Basil of Caesarea: A Guide to his Life and Doctrine* (Eugene, OR: Cascade Books, 2012), 121–32.

[10]*Exhortatoria ad sanctum baptisma* (=*Bapt.*, also identified as *Hom.* 13).

sermon by Gregory of Nazianzus, *Or.* 40, can be dated to January 6, 381.[11] Basil draws on the celebration of Jesus' baptism by John in the Jordan River to craft an impassioned plea for adult catechumens to stop procrastinating and sign up to be baptized at Easter. Many, if not most of those raised in the Church during this period were lifelong catechumens, putting off baptism until they might reasonably expect to live in such a way as to avoid falling into sin. What this meant in practice was that people were baptized only when they decided to take up an ascetic life, or when they got sick and feared they would soon die. Basil argues against this practice by insisting that one is spiritually safer *with* baptism at any stage in life, and that it will in fact help in the struggle against sin. To postpone baptism is to take a serious risk of missing out on salvation altogether, since one never knows when death will strike, or if one will be capable of rational participation in the last hours.

Two Homilies On Fasting[12]

Basil's two sermons on fasting, preached during the season of Lent, are characteristic of his broader focus on community identity in their emphasis on fasting as a beneficial tool that can build and support a healthy civic and social order. Fasting, he says, should not be an act of self-righteous perfection, but part of a godly moral concern for the good of others and the good of the city.[13] Many early Christian Greek sermons on fasting survive from the ancient world, including a large number of anonymous or pseudonymous texts preserved in the

[11]Jean Bernardi, *La Prédication des Pères Cappadociens: Le Prédicateur et son auditoire* (Publications de la faculté des lettres et sciences humaines de l'Université de Montpellier 30; Montpellier: Presses Universitaires de France, 1968), 68. See Burnett Comings, *Aspects of the Liturgical Year in Cappadocia*, 73–82 for discussion of Gregory of Nazianzus' and Gregory of Nyssa's sermons on baptism.

[12]*De ieiunio* 1 and 2 (=*Iei 1, Iei 2*, also known in some traditional collections of Basil's sermons as *Hom.* 1 and *Hom.* 2).

[13]The sermons suggest that Basil expected his audience to practice a five-day fast each week (Mondays through Fridays) during Lent.

collections of leading preachers such as Basil and John Chrysostom. The two translated here are those found most consistently in Basil's works. Some doubt Basil's authorship of the second sermon (often found first in many manuscripts). Regardless of its authenticity, the second homily appears to be a slightly disorganized short version of many details also found in the first.

Such sermons would have served as models to guide other preachers, who often copied them or adapted them to circumstance, including paraphrases in other languages such as Latin, Syriac, and Coptic. The Roman monk Rufinus, for example, freely adapted Basil's sermons on fasting in his own Latin "translations."[14] Lenten sermons on fasting were often also associated with sermons preaching other types of ascetic divestment, such as almsgiving or care for the poor. For example, we know that Ambrose in Milan lifted and paraphrased sections from Basil's sermon against usury in his Latin sermon on Tobit.[15] Gregory of Nyssa also drew from Basil's sermon against usury in his own homily on usury after his brother's death.[16]

Homily Against Drunkards[17]

Basil's sermon against drunkenness was perhaps not quite what his Christian audience expected to hear when they turned up in church for the celebration of the Easter festival. Easter sermons by the fourth century began on the festival itself and would have continued over the next week for the "Easter Octave." This sermon is perhaps one of

[14]H. Marti, "Rufinus' Translation of St. Basil's Sermon on Fasting," *Studia Patristica* 16 (1985): 418–22. For the Latin text and a German translation, see Heinrich Marti, *Rufin von Aquileia: De Ieiunio I, II: Zwei Predigten über das Fasten nach Basileios von Kaisareia.* Vigiliae Christianae Supplements 6. Leiden: Brill, 1989.

[15]Holman, *The Hungry are Dying,* 101, 124.

[16]For discussion, see now Brenda Llewellyn Ihssen, *They Who Give from Evil: The Response of the Eastern Church to Moneylending in the Early Christian Era* (Eugene, OR: Pickwick Publications, 2012).

[17]*In Ebriosos* (=*Ebr.*, also known as *Hom.* 14).

Basil's most searing extended diatribes against any particular behavior, as he reacts to the apparently unbridled inebriation with which some Christians were celebrating the feast in Caesarea.

Easter marked a fixed point for contrast, as Christians turned from Lenten fasting, with its focus on drinking only water, to their usual use of the mildly alcoholic beverages such as wine that were standard fare (and likely often safer than water) in the ancient urban world. In Cappadocia, evidently, some had taken this liberty to an extreme at the earliest possible moment, turning up in church ready for wild dancing rather than rational praise and prayer. Such association between festival and inebriation is timeless,[18] and it is not surprising that this sermon has had a universal appeal, widely translated into popular languages across the centuries.

In response, Basil uses the Easter pulpit to appeal for a Christian lifestyle that better respects moderation and the reasoning mind. As he does in his discussion of grief, in his homilies *On Giving Thanks* (see below), Basil affirms that wine has its good uses; there is no sin in drinking. But the weakness that follows excess is not just a door to sin, but also unhealthy. As with mourning, one should also celebrate in a spirit of temperance and moderation, with respect for wine's power to heal and to warm and encourage the spirits, but only if used properly.

On Giving Thanks[19] and *On the Martyr Julitta*[20]

Basil preached the two sermons, *On Giving Thanks* and *On the Martyr Julitta*, which he treats as a unified message delivered over two days, the day before and the day of this martyr's feast in July,[21]

---

[18]The modern practice was illustrated poignantly by an online Twitterfeed "tweet" I saw from Christmas Eve 2012 that read, "Time to get drunk and go to church."

[19]*De gratiarum actione* (=*Grat.*, also known as *Hom. 4*).

[20]*In martyrem Julittam* (=*Iul.*, also known as *Hom. 5*).

[21]For an immensely helpful table of the calendar of saints in the Cappadocians,

at or near the site of her tomb in the main church at Caesarea. Taken together, they provide an extended study on 1 Thessalonians 5.16–18, "Rejoice always, pray without ceasing, give thanks in all circumstances." His panegyric on Julitta herself—a mere two chapters at the beginning of the second sermon—is witness to a tradition that venerated an early Christian woman who spoke boldly about men and women's equality in spiritual abilities, courage, and related virtues. Scholars have tended to focus on Julitta's example as it relates to gender studies in early Christianity.[22] But Basil's extensive moral exhortation on thanksgiving and tears in difficult circumstances, which profoundly shapes the context in which he tells her story, has received virtually no attention in patristic studies up to now.

This failure to connect the two messages is partly Basil's fault, since he jumps abruptly from one to the other. In his hurry at the end of 5.2, he says, in essence, "So much for the incomparable Julitta. Let's get back to what I was talking about yesterday!" Yet Julitta's story illustrates precisely the type of exuberant joy in times of trial and consolatory flow of healing waters in bereavement that Basil wishes to convey throughout his message on thanksgiving. In fact, his exposition of the Thessalonians passage might also be said to summarize the full range of Basil's views on how one ought to approach both feasts and fasts.

The incomparable Julitta was a local woman in Caesarea whose substantial property holdings were threatened by a swindler's lawsuit during the pre-Constantinian persecutions against Christians. When her opponent exposed her faith at the trial, she eagerly

see Limberis, *Architects of Piety*, 42, Table 1.1, where Julitta's feastday is given as July 30. Other sources variously date the feast to July 15 or even June 16 (Burnett Comings, *Aspects of the Liturgical Year in Cappadocia*, 103).

[22]See, for example, Philip M. Beagon, "The Cappadocian Fathers, Women and Ecclesiastical Politics," *Vigiliae Christianae* 49.2 (May 1995): 165–79; Verna E.F. Harrison, "Male and Female in Cappadocian Theology," *Journal of Theological Studies* NS 42, part 2 (October 1990): 441–71; Johan Leemans, "Preaching Christian Virtue: Basil of Caesarea's Panegyrical Sermon on Julitta," *Virtutis Imago: Studies on the Conceptualisation and Transformation of an Ancient Ideal*, 259–84, Gert Partoens, Geert Roskam, and Toon Van Houdt, eds., Leuven: Peeters, 2004; Limberis, *Architects of Piety*, esp. pp. 203–7; and James C. Skedros, "The Cappadocian Fathers on the Veneration of Martyrs," *Studia Patristica* 37 (1999): 294–300, esp. 295.

threw over all claim to her wealth. Her confession so infuriated the judge that he condemned her to death. Before leaping into the fire, however, Julitta took the public opportunity to address the women present at her trial, offering them strong words of exhortation and courage. Men too, says Basil, should take her words to heart and not fall short of this woman's example.

Julitta is a woman very much alone in this sermon. Her age is unknown and no husband or children are mentioned, although it is generally assumed that she was a widow. As her story took various forms in popular piety over the following centuries, it was often conflated with an otherwise unknown and generally considered apocryphal woman also named Julitta, mother of a young boy (Cyr or Cyriacus) martyred at Antioch. While the trials in the story might seem, to Basil's audience, to belong to the distant past, in fact Basil's episcopate dates to a period known for Neo-Arian tensions that were often regarded as another form of "persecution," described in several of Basil's letters during the 370s.[23] We do not know if these difficulties had any bearing for his audience here.

Basil on Tears, Consolation, and Gratitude

Basil is all too aware that, as William Butler Yeats once put it, "The world's more full of weeping than we can understand."[24] Basil uses these two sermons to consider, in pastoral terms, how it is possible to practice perpetual joy, prayer, and thanksgiving in the face of life's uncertainties, sorrows, and loss. Repeatedly emphasizing that it is

[23]Leemans, "Preaching Christian Virtue," 275–6. Basil describes events, in his *Ep.* 243 written to beg help from the bishops of Italy and Gaul in 376, that included clerical oppression, church seizures, exiles, "flight of presbyters, flight of deacons, and harassing of all the clergy." It was, he said, "the most oppressive of persecutions . . . because the persecutors are cloaked with the name of Christians." Basil of Caesarea, *Basil: Letters,* Deferrari, trans., Loeb Classical Library (Cambridge, MA: Harvard University Press, 1930), 3.439, 3.437.

[24]W.B. Yeats, "The Stolen Child," *The Collected Poems of W.B. Yeats*, rev. 2nd edn., Richard J. Finneran, ed. (New York: Simon & Schuster, 1996), 18–19.

possible, Basil considers a range of specific situations and imagined responses and objections. He draws much on medical imagery throughout his writings, and here we find this in the way he comments on the proper Christian practice of tears.

Kimberley Patton has identified three kinds of weeping in early Christian texts: the supernatural "gift of tears" (a personal mark of sanctity for a select few), tears that signify repentance, and tears that may be "shed out of sorrow for the fallen state of the world" to express both indignation and compassion.[25] Basil's concern in these sermons is on the third type. He contrasts worldly self-centered tears (and joy) with an ideal Christian response based on empathy for others and trust in eternal securities. Proper weeping is important for good health, he says. Those who are overwhelmed by calamity, but have never been able to "evaporate" their sorrow through weeping face serious risk of apoplexy and paralysis, and some, he says, have died from failing to release these pressures.

Such healing may also occur as a natural result of allowing tears to play a vital role in consoling others. Weeping with those who weep, Basil says, is a gift to God, expressing charitable lovingkindness (*philostorgia*) to one's neighbor. It can also open the way to proper penitential weeping, and build godly virtue and joy. Such consolatory weeping must be gentle, just as a soothing touch on one with a fever helps to disperse the inner illness. Here the sermon would naturally have reminded the original audience of the festal focus on the miraculous spring there in the church precincts that, according to tradition, burst forth at Julitta's tomb. Its waters were compared with a mother's milk and were collected by the faithful for medicinal purposes and spiritual comfort. While her joyful leap into the fire transformed her from mortal to an indestructible source of living waters, those who cannot weep may (he says) be destroyed by an internal fire, or hardened against showing others proper compassion.

[25]Kimberley Christine Patton and John Stratton Hawley, eds., *Holy Tears: Weeping in the Religious Imagination* (Princeton: Princeton University Press, 2005), 1.

Basil's emphasis on this modulation of self-control in expressing celebration and tempered sobriety is a common theme that runs through all of the sermons in this volume. And Basil's support of tears reflects a common theme in other patristic texts.[26] Gregory of Nazianzus, for example, emphasizes tears in describing his mother's prayers at the church altar where she died.[27] Gregory of Nyssa described his sister, Macrina, mixing her tears with dirt at the altar during a night of prayer for healing of a breast tumor.[28] And Nazianzen's sister, Gorgonia, similarly anointed her whole body with tears during a night at the church altar seeking healing. Instead of earth, Gorgonia dared to use "a portion of the consecrated precious Body and Blood which she treasured in her hand, and with which she mingled her tears."[29]

Basil also draws from his teachings on self-control and gratitude to advance his view of God's gifts as tools for the present life and our relationships with one another in all of our needs. In chapter seven of his sermon on Julitta, he writes, for example, "Those assets given to

[26]It also agrees with some aspects of Jewish rabbinic tradition, which was taking shape during this period, for example, the tradition that Moses wrote the last verses of the Pentateuch literally with his own tears as he lay dying, as one scholar puts it, "sealing his life and his book in the only manner it could be sealed, with the divine ocular fluid, the viscosity of which formed the letters . . . facing the other weeping face, in the work of compassion that must come to close but is always open." Rabbi Nehemia Polen, "Divine Weeping on Mount Nebo," Patton and Hawley, eds., *Holy Tears*, 90.

[27]See e.g., Gregory of Nazianzus, *Epigrams* 24–75, W.R. Paton, ed. and trans., *The Greek Anthology, Books 7–8*, Loeb Classical Library (Cambridge, MA: Harvard University Press, 1917), 410–31.

[28]Gregory of Nyssa, *Life of Macrina*, PG 46, 989–992; see Virginia Woods Callahan, ed., "Vita S. Macrinae," W. Jaeger, ed., *Gregorii Nysseni Opera 8.1. Gregorii Nysseni Opera Ascetica* (Leiden: Brill, 1952), 404–6; Virginia Woods Callahan, trans., "The Life of Saint Macrina," in Callahan, ed. and trans., *Saint Gregory of Nyssa: Ascetical Works*, Fathers of the Church (Washington, DC: Catholic University of America Press, 1967), 185. See also Georgia Frank, "Macrina's Scar: Homeric Allusions and Heroic Identity in Gregory of Nyssa's *Life of Macrina*," *Journal of Early Christian Studies* 8.4 (Winter 2000): 511–30.

[29]Gregory of Nazianzus, *Life of Gorgonia* 18; see "On His Sister, St. Gorgonia," Leo P. McCauley, trans., *Funeral Orations by Saint Gregory Nazianzen and Saint Ambrose*, Fathers of the Church (Washington, DC: Catholic University of America Press, 1953), 113–14.

you, advance them by your alms through the hand of the poor, and though he has received his own property, so it is a perfect thanks, as if you have given from your own goods." Joy, prayer, and thanks must interact in all circumstances in a cycle of perpetual exchange, healing, and consolation.

On the Holy Martyr Mamas

In contrast with Basil's careful development of ideas about thanks-giving, his sermon on the martyr saint-shepherd, Mamas, reads as if he was forced into the pulpit and is improvising with all his might. The sermon says nothing about Mamas' life or the circumstances of his martyrdom and veneration beyond the bare fact that he was a shepherd. The sermon is more explicit about the practice of his veneration: he is frequently invoked in song, prayers, on tombs, for voyages, and in sickness, including miraculously reviving infants from death and prolonging life. Basil explicitly says he is preaching at the very turn of a new year, which is commonly interpreted to mean September 2, but Richard Burgess has suggested was actually October 3 at this time in Cappadocia.[30]

We have some hints about this festival at Caesarea preserved by the eleventh-century Archbishop Nicetas of Heraclea, a lead-ing medieval commentator on Gregory of Nazianzus' sermon *On New Sunday*, which was preached at the spring festival for this

[30]Professor Burgess noted some years ago that the new year in fourth-century Cappadocia occurred in early October (and not September 1, as is commonly believed), since "the Antiochene calendar didn't change its new year from 1 October (1 Hyperberetaios) to 1 September (1 Gorpaios) until some time between 458 and 483 (long after Basil)"; R.W. Burgess, correspondence posted online at the LtAntiq listserv, accessed June 6, 2000. Talley makes a similar point in *Origins of the Liturgical Year*, 96. For a general discussion, see chapter three in R. W. Burgess, *Studies in Eusebian and Post-Eusebian Chronology. 1 The Chronici Canones of Eusebius of Caesarea: Structure, Content and Chronology, AD 282–325; 2 The Continuatio Antiochiensis Eusebii: A Chronicle of Antioch and the Roman Near East during the Reigns of Constantine and Constantius II, AD 325–50*; Historia Einzelschriften 135 (Stuttgart: Franz Steiner, 1999).

same martyr. According to Nicetas, tradition placed his martyrdom around 275, and Nazianzus' playful comment about some at the festival "grudging" his delivery of the sermon in the martyrium at Caesarea may suggest that Basil himself was present.[31] If this is correct, Brian Daley suggests, it would date Gregory's sermon to the mid 370s. The shrine itself had been constructed for the martyr by the future emperor, Julian, and his half-brother, Gallus, likely in the early 350s.

Basil begins and ends his sermon with an extended apology, begging the audience for tolerance of his weakness and inadequacy to the task. Such apology was a common trope in Roman rhetoric, but here seems somewhat overdone; perhaps he was relieved to ask Gregory to preach the sermon on a spring celebration of the feast.

As with the sermon on Julitta, Basil again here uses the opportunity to turn the focus away from the festal martyr onto something more theological, in this case warning the audience against false doctrine about the divinity of Christ. Chapter four, which takes up nearly half of the sermon, builds on biblical examples of shepherd-leaders, to focus on Jesus' teaching of himself as the good shepherd. In an extended warning against "false shepherds," Basil alludes to those who lead believers astray through twisted interpretations of Christ's essence (*ousia*), *hypostasis*, and relationship with God the Father. *On the Holy Martyr Mamas* is not the only sermon to link this figure with the Trinitarian controversy. Gregory's *Sermon on New Sunday*, for example, implicitly connects them in its central focus on the Easter light of the Trinity.[32] Another homily surviving in six manuscripts of Basil's work also appears to be a merged adaptation of these themes, titled, *De Trinitate et in martyrem Mamantem*.[33]

[31]Cited in Brian Daley, *Gregory of Nazianzus* (New York: Routledge, 2006), 155. Daley finds no support for the common scholarly view that dates Gregory's *Sermon on New Sunday* to after Basil's death.

[32]Christopher A. Beeley, *Gregory of Nazianzus on the Trinity and the Knowledge of God: In Your Light We Shall See Light*, Oxford Studies in Historical Theology (New York: Oxford University Press, 2008), 59.

[33]Cited and briefly described in Paul Jonathan Fedwick, *Bibliotheca Basiliana*

On the Martyr Barlaam

The sermon on the martyr Barlaam is traditionally included in collections of Basil's homilies, but the general consensus is that someone else wrote it. It is one of four known surviving texts on this little-known martyr, a man celebrated for his self-control when forced to hold a burning libation in his bare hands, who resisted to the end the pressure to drop it and so make an involuntary sacrifice to the Roman deities. Wendy Mayer, who translated John Chrysostom's sermon on Barlaam, dates his festival to either May 31 or August 14.[34] Another Greek homily on Barlaam, by Severus of Antioch (surviving only in Syriac translation), was preached in 515.[35] The homily by Pseudo-Basil translated in this volume places the saint's tomb locally, but since we don't know the real author we can't say where that was; in or near Antioch is most likely. The fourth text, a passion narrative rather than a homily, survives in several manuscripts.[36] This text (in which the feast is dated to November 16) belongs to the genre tradition of martyrdom trial transcripts, rough and anonymous verbatim exchanges (real and imagined) between the accused and the governor or judge who decides their fate.[37]

Vniversalis: A Study of the Manuscript Tradition, Translations and Editions of the Works of Basil of Caesarea. II. The Homiliae Morales, Hexaemeron, De Letteris, with Additional Coverage of the Letters (2 vols.). Corpus Chrisianorum. Turnhout: Brepols, 1996, vol. 1, p. 1210.

[34]John Chrysostom, "On Saint Barlaam," trans. Wendy Mayer, in Wendy Mayer with Bronwen Neil, *St. John Chrysostom: The Cult of the Saints* (Yonkers, NY: St Vladimir Seminary Press, 2006), 177–89.

[35]Severus of Antioch, *Hom.* 73. trans. Maurice Brière, *Patrologia Orientalia* 12 (1919): 90–6.

[36]For an early study on this text with translation in Portuguese, see Francisco Maria Esteves Pereira, *O Santo Martyr Barlaam: Estudio de Critica historica* (Coimbra [Portugal]: Imprensa da Universidade, 1901). For a critical edition of the Greek and extended discussion, see Hippolyte Delehaye, "S. Barlaam: Martyr à Antioche," *Analecta Bollandiana* 22 (1903): 129–45. For a broader discussion of the cult of martyrs, see also Hippolyte Delehaye, *Les origines du culte des martyrs*, Subsidia Hagiographica 20 (Brussels: Société des Bollandistes, 1933).

[37]For other examples in this style from second and third-century Christian martyrdom accounts, see Herbert Musurillo, *The Acts of the Christian Martyrs* (Oxford:

The key elements of Barlaam's story are the same in all four texts. An ordinary man from the country, he was arrested as a Christian and asked to prove his political loyalty by sacrifice. When he refused, he was forced to hold out his hand over a makeshift altar, and a lump of burning incense was dropped into his palm. When he defied the plot by permitting the coal to burn into his flesh while never letting the incense drop, his endurance enraged the officials, who brought a quick end to his life. The story is told in excruciating detail, emphasizing the power of Christian endurance, and martyrdom as a moral athletic competition over evil. As in the sermon on Mamas, Barlaam's lowly origins are part of the essential message praising his spiritual strength and the power of his example. Following a common rhetorical device in festal sermons, the homilist treats the saint as if personally present, welcoming the crowds and hosting the party.

* * *

This book began more than ten years ago, as part of a (literal) holiday excursion into the modern translation history of Basil's minor sermons on feasts and fasts. Its slow progress (the nature of holidays) meant that, to my great delight, several of the longer texts originally envisioned within the project have been published in superb English translations by other scholars in the interim, and therefore are not included here.[38] When family circumstances forced further delay,

Clarendon Press, 1972, repr. 1999); and Musurillo, *The Acts of the Pagan Martyrs: Acta Alexandrinorum* (Oxford: Clarendon Press, 1954, repr. 1999).

[38]See, e.g., Pauline Allen's translation of Basil's homilies *On the Martyr Gordius* and *On the Forty Martyrs of Sebaste*, in Johan Leemans, Wendy Mayer, Pauline Allen, and Boudewijn Dehandschutter, eds., *'Let us Die that We May Live': Greek Homilies on Christian Martyrs from Asia Minor, Palestine and Syria (c. AD 350–AD 450)* (London and New York: Routledge, 2003), 56–77. I have chosen to retain here my slightly more paraphrastic rendering of *On the Martyr Barlaam*, since the text of Professor Allen's recent translation came to my attention late and may not be available to most readers; see Pauline Allen, "Loquacious Locals: Two Indigenous Martyrs in the Homilies of Severus of Antioch," In J. Leemans, ed., *Martyrdom and Persecution in Late Antique*

I was very pleased to learn that Mark DelCogliano had complete manuscript translations prepared on the homily *On the Holy Birth of Christ,* the two homilies *On Fasting,* and *Homily Against Drunkards.* I thank Mark for his willingness to agree to publication in a joint volume, and his patience and good cheer throughout the process; the book is much enriched by the inclusion of these four texts in his distinct voice. We have prepared our translations separately, with occasional minor consultation but each reflecting and preserving individual style and preferences. Research on two sermons, *On Giving Thanks* and *On the Martyr Julitta,* further benefited from discussion in a short communication session at the Oxford International Patristic Conference in 2011. Any errors that remain are my own. Finally, I am deeply grateful to the community of Holy Trinity Orthodox Cathedral in Boston, its Rector and Dean, the Very Rev. Robert M. Arida, and its magnificent mosaic iconostasis panel of Basil, Gregory of Nazianzus, and John Chrysostom, which have consistently helped to keep me focused.

Susan R. Holman
January 1, 2013
Feast of St Basil

Christianity: Festschrift Boudewijn Dehandschutter, Bibliotheca Ephemeridum Theologicarum Lovaniensium 241 (Leuven: Peeters, 2010), 11–14.

On the Holy Birth of Christ[1]

1 Revere in silence that birth of Christ which was first and fitting and proper to his divinity. We should keep our mind from searching into it or being inquisitive about it. For when no time nor age comes between them,[2] when there is no way to imagine things, no spectator present, no narrator, how can the intellect even form a thought? How can the tongue serve the mind? Indeed, the Father was and the Son was born. Do not say, "When?" That's a stupid question. Do not ask, "How?" An answer is impossible. For "when" has temporal overtones and "how" makes us slide toward corporeal ways of conceptualizing his birth. I can say only what Scripture says: as radiance from glory and as an image from the archetype.[3] But since this rationale for responding to such questions does not put an end to your inquisitive thoughts, I take refuge in the ineffability of its glory. I acknowledge that the manner in which the divine birth took place is incomprehensible to human thoughts and impossible to express with human words. Do not say, "If he was born, he was not."[4] Do not wickedly seize upon the vulgar interpretation of these

[1]This translation is based on the edition of Luigi Gambero, *L'omelia sulla generazione di Cristo di Basilo di Cesarea. Il posto della vergine Maria*, Marian Studies Library n.s. 13–14 (Dayton: University of Dayton, 1981–1982), 177–200. The classic edition by Julien Garnier can be found in Gabriel Rudolf Ludwig De Sinner (ed.), *Sancti Patris nostri Basilii, Caesareae Cappadociae archiepiscopi, opera omnia quae exstant*, Editio Parisina altera, emendata et aucta (Paris: Gaume Fratres, 1839), vol. 2, 848–858, as well as PG 31, 1457–1476. The notes on this homily by Fronto du Duc (Ducaeus) can be found in De Sinner, vol. 2, 1111–4.
[2]I.e., between the Father and Son. The thought here is that since the Son's birth from the Father is non-temporal, the human mind, which can operate only in a temporal manner, is unsuited for understanding it.
[3]See Heb 1.3.
[4]This of course is a version of what Arius is supposed to have claimed: it logically

words,[5] corrupting the truth and defiling the divine teaching[6] on the basis of examples here below. I said, "he was born," so that I could indicate his origin and cause, not so that I could expose the Only Begotten as posterior to time. Do not allow your intellect to tumble into the pitfall of making the ages prior to the Son, seeing that they did not yet exist nor had yet to come into being. For how can things that have been made be prior to the one who made them?[7] But I see that unawares I have gotten into what I wanted to avoid in the course of this sermon. So then, let us put aside talk about that eternal and ineffable birth, realizing that our intellect is quite unequal to understanding such realities and our speech quite insufficient for expressing such thoughts.[8]

2 So then, we must consider how far we fall when we move from the truth itself to speaking about the truth. Even though the intellect cannot ascend to the nature of incomprehensible realities, it is still impossible to find a mode of discourse that communicates whatever it does think.[9] God is upon the earth. God is among human beings.[10] He does not establish the Law by fire and trumpet and smoking mountain,[11] nor by thick darkness and a gloom and a storm that frightens the souls of those who hear it.[12] Instead, by means of a body he engages in gentle and pleasant conversation with those who are

follows from the fact of the Son's birth that the Son did not exist before he was born. Pro-Nicene theologians such as Basil denied that the Son's birth implied a beginning to his existence; see Basil's treatise against Eunomius, *Eun.* 2.11–17.

[5]I.e. the words "he was born," not the sentence, "If he was born, he was not."

[6]Gk. θεολογία. For Basil, "divine teaching" or "theology" (θεολογία) is the account concerned with Christ's eternal divine being in abstraction from his works. It is distinct from the account concerned with the "economy" (οἰκονομία) of Christ's saving actions, which Basil will deal with in the remainder of this homily. On θεολογία, see *Eun.* 2.3 and 2.15.

[7]See Heb 1.2.

[8]This first paragraph summarizes several themes in Book 2 of *Eun.*

[9]Cf. *Epistle* 7 and *Fide* 1–2, where Basil also speaks of language as an imperfect vehicle for human thoughts about God.

[10]Cf. Bar 3.38.

[11]See Ex 20.18.

[12]See Deut 4.11; 5.22; Heb 12.18–19.

the same in kind.[13] God is in flesh. He is not active at intervals as he was among the prophets. Instead he possesses a humanity[14] connatural and united to himself, and restores all humanity[15] to himself through flesh the same as ours in kind.[16]

So then, one might say, "How did the splendor come to all by means of one?[17] How can divinity come to be in flesh?" As fire comes to be in iron: not by a change of place, but by a sharing of itself.[18] For the fire does not go out of itself and into the iron; rather, while remaining in its place, it shares its own power with the iron. It is in no way diminished when it shares itself, and the whole of it fills whatever shares in it. So it is in this way too that God the Word did not move out of himself when *he dwelt among us.*[19] Nor did he undergo a change when *the Word became flesh.*[20] Heaven was not deprived of what it contained, and earth received the heavenly one within its own embraces. Do not suppose that the divinity fell. For it did not move from one place to another as bodies do. Do not imagine that the divinity was altered when it was transferred into flesh. For the immortal is immutable.

So then, one might ask, "How was God the Word not filled with bodily weakness?" We reply: as the fire does not share in the distinguishing marks of the iron. Iron is black and cold, but nonetheless when turned in the fire it takes on the outward form of fire. The iron glows, yet the fire is not blackened. The iron is set ablaze, yet it does not cool the flame. So too it is with the human flesh of the Lord: it shares in the divinity, yet it does not impart its own weakness to the divinity. Can it be that you did not grant to the divinity an activity on par with that of this mortal fire? Did you imagine passibility in

[13] Gk. ὁμογενής.
[14] Gk. τὸ ἄνθρωπον.
[15] Gk. τὴν ἀνθρωπότητα.
[16] Gk. συγγενής.
[17] Basil probably means "one body."
[18] It is impossible to capture the wordplay here: *ou metabatikōs, alla metadotikōs.*
[19] Jn 1.14.
[20] Ibid.

the impassible one on the basis of human weakness? Are you puzzled how the easily corruptible nature can have incorruptibility through its communion with God? Realize that it's a mystery. God is in flesh that he may kill the death that lurks therein. For as the harm caused by poisonous drugs can be overcome by antidotes when they are assimilated by the body, and as the darkness residing in a house is dissolved by the introduction of light, so too the death that dominates in human nature is obliterated by the presence of divinity. And as ice in water, for as long as it is night and dark, is stronger than the liquid that contains it, but the warming sun melts the ice by its ray, so too death rules until the advent of Christ, but when *the saving grace of God appears*[21] and *the sun of righteousness rises,*[22] *death is swallowed up in victory,*[23] unable to bear the visitation of true life.

O the depth of the goodness of God and his love for humanity! In response to his superabundant love for humanity we rebel against being his servants.[24] We seek to know the reason why God is among humans, though we should be adoring his goodness.

3 O human, what should we do with you? When God remains in the heights, you do not seek him. When he comes down and converses with you through flesh, you do not receive him. But how will you be brought into affinity with God when you seek explanations? Realize that God is in flesh for this reason: because the flesh that was cursed needed to be sanctified, the flesh that was weakened needed to be strengthened, the flesh that was alienated from God needed to be brought into affinity with him, the flesh that had fallen in paradise needed to be led back into heaven.

And what is the workshop for this divine economy?[25] The body of the Holy Virgin. Who is responsible for the birth? The Holy

[21]Titus 2.11.
[22]Mal 4.2.
[23]1 Cor 15.54.
[24]Cf. *Chr.* 6.
[25]Gk. οἰκονομία. Fronto du Duc's description of this term remains accurate today: "In using this term, the Fathers designate not only his taking of our flesh, but

Spirit and the Power of the Most High who overshadowed her.[26] [To answer these questions] even better, listen to what the Gospel says: *When his mother Mary had been betrothed to Joseph, before they came together, she was found to be with child of the Holy Spirit.*[27] Even though she was betrothed to a man, the Virgin was judged suitable for service in this economy, such that virginity would be honored and marriage not disparaged. While virginity was chosen as suitable for holiness, the initial phases of marriage were included through the betrothal. At the same time, so that Joseph could witness Mary's purity with his own eyes and she would not be subjected to ridicule as if she had defiled her virginity, she was given a betrothed who would defend her character.[28] I must also mention another reason that is no less honorable than those already stated: the suitable time for the incarnation[29] of the Lord was predestined long ago and prearranged *before the foundation of the world.*[30] It occurred when it was appropriate for the Holy Spirit and the Power of the Most High to form that God-bearing[31] flesh. Since the human race down to Mary did not have a purity that matched hers in honor, such that it could receive the Holy Spirit's activity, the Blessed Virgin had been betrothed in anticipation of her being chosen for this, and the betrothal did not harm her virginity. But one of the ancients

also all the other aspects of the office of Christ the Lord as our Redeemer, such as his preaching, passion, resurrection, and ascension" (De Sinner, vol. 2, 1111). See also note 6 above.

[26]See Lk 1.35.

[27]Mt 1.18.

[28]See Origen, *Homilies on Luke* 6.3.

[29]Gk. ἐνανθρώπησις, literally, "becoming human," or "inhumanization."

[30]1 Pet 1.20; cf. Jn 17.24.

[31]Basil also calls Christ's flesh θεοφόρος (*theophoros*, "God-bearing") in *Spir.* 5.12 and *Ps59* 4. The thesis that Christ was a God-bearing man was condemned as Nestorian in the fifth of the twelve anathemas which Cyril appended to his third letter to Nestorius (Cyril, *Epistle* 17). This letter was included in the Acts of the Council of Ephesus, though not formally approved by the council fathers. Cyril's *Epistle* 17, along with *Epistles* 4 and 39, quickly became viewed as standard expressions of Christological orthodoxy. Some manuscripts of this homily read *Christophoros* instead of *Theophoros*. This is probably an intentional alteration made by a scribe concerned to bring Basil into step with a later Christological orthodoxy.

mentions another reason, that the betrothal to Joseph was intended to conceal Mary's virginity from *the ruler of this age*.[32] The external form of the betrothal to the Virgin was intended to be a kind of decoy for the wicked one. For he kept an eye on virgins for a long time, from the moment he heard the Prophet say: *Behold, a virgin shall conceive and bear a son*.[33] So then, he who hoped to ambush virginity was deceived by the betrothal. After all, he knew that his dominion would end when the Lord was manifested in the flesh.

4   *Before they came together, she was found to be with child of the Holy Spirit*.[34] It was Joseph who discovered both of these things, that she had conceived and what caused her to conceive, that it was *of the Holy Spirit*. And so, fearing to be called the husband of such a woman, *he resolved to divorce her quietly*.[35] For he did not have the stomach to publicize what had happened to her. But *being a righteous man*,[36] he obtained a revelation of the mysteries. *For as he considered these things, an angel of the Lord appeared to him in a dream, saying: Do not fear to take Mary as your wife*.[37] Do not think that he was trying to conceal some sin of hers in the face of absurd conjectures. For he was called *a righteous man*, and he who is righteous does not conceal transgressions through silence. *Do not fear to take Mary as your wife*. This shows that neither was he vexed at her nor did he feel loathing for her; rather, it indicates that he feared to take her because she was filled with the Holy Spirit. *For that which has been born in her is of the Holy Spirit*.[38] And here it is clear that the Lord's frame did not come into existence as does the ordinary nature of the flesh. For what she was pregnant with was immediately perfect in the flesh,

[32]1 Cor 2.6, 8. This "one of the ancients" is Ignatius of Antioch, who wrote: "And the virginity of Mary was concealed from the ruler of this age" (*Epistle to the Ephesians* 19.1). Here Basil has borrowed from Origen, *Homilies on Luke* 6.4.

[33]Is 7.14.
[34]Mt 1.18.
[35]Mt 1.19.
[36]Ibid.
[37]Mt 1.20.
[38]Mt 1.20.

not formed through incremental stages of construction, as is clear from the words themselves.[39] For it did not say: "that which has been created," but *that which has been born*. So then, since the flesh was formed from holiness, it was worthy of being united to the divinity of the Only Begotten.[40]

And she will bear a son, and you shall call his name Jesus.[41] We have observed that names purposely imposed indicate the nature of those to whom they refer, as in the case of Abraham, Isaac, and Israel. For the designation given to each of these men does not intimate their bodily characteristic but rather the distinguishing mark of the virtuous deed accomplished by each of them.[42] Therefore, in the present case he is designated "Jesus"—that is, salvation of the people.[43] It is at this point that the mystery appointed before the ages and announced long ago by the prophets had its fulfillment.[44] *Behold, a virgin shall conceive and bear a son, and they shall call his name "Emmanuel," which translated means "God with us."*[45] Long ago this very designation disclosed the whole mystery of God's being among human beings, when it says that *Emmanuel* is interpreted *God with us*.

And no one should be misled by the captiousness of the Jews, who claim the Prophet used the word "maiden" instead of "virgin," as in, "Behold, a maiden shall conceive."[46] In the first place, it is a

---

[39]Basil's terminology here is medical. In *Eun.* 2.5 he described the stages of in utero development: "there is sexual intercourse of a male with a female, then conception in the womb, then construction, then formation, and then at the right time passage to the outside world." "Construction" refers to the seed's development into the embryo, and "formation" to the articulation of the embryo into a recognizably human fetus.

[40]Basil also speaks of Christ's body being "formed" (συμπαγεῖσα) in *Spir.* 5.12.

[41]Mt 1.21.

[42]This theory of proper names, i.e. what proper names signify about the people whom bear them, is consistent with the theory articulated in *Eun.* 2.4.

[43]Cf. Mt 1.21.

[44]Cf. Mt 1.22.

[45]Mt 1.23.

[46]There was a long-standing debate between Christians and Jews over whether the Hebrew word *'almah* in Is 7.14 should be translated into Greek as παρθένος

mark of the utmost irrationality to think that what the Lord gave as a sign could be something so ordinary and taken for granted by everyone. For what does the Prophet say? *And again the Lord spoke to Ahaz, saying: "Ask a sign from the Lord your God, in the depth or in the height." And Ahaz said: "I will not ask, and I will not put the Lord to the test!"*[47] Then a little bit after he said: *Therefore the Lord himself will give you a sign. Behold, the virgin shall conceive.*[48] Seeing that Ahaz did not ask a sign *in the depth or in the height,*[49] so that you could learn that *he who descended to the lower parts of the earth is he who ascended above all the heavens,*[50] the Lord himself gave a sign. And this sign is something incredible and wonderful, and quite contrary to the ordinary nature of things. The same woman is both a virgin and a mother, remaining in the holy condition of her virginity while allotted the blessing of childbearing. But if some have rendered it "maiden" instead of "virgin" based on their interpretation of the Hebrew term, nothing is ruined by using this word. For we have found in the customary usage of Scripture that "maiden" is often used instead of "virgin." For example, in Deuteronomy it says: *If a man meets a young virgin who is not betrothed, and seizes her and lies with her, and he is found, then the man who lay with her shall give to the father of the maiden fifty double-drachmas.*[51]

5 *And when Joseph woke from sleep, he took her as his wife.*[52] He undertook his marriage with the disposition that is incumbent upon

("virgin"), as it had in the Septuagint, or as νεᾶνις ("maiden"), as other Jewish translators insisted. While the church fathers insisted on the correctness of the Septuagint translation (and Jerome translated the term by *virgo* in the Latin Vulgate), modern translations corroborate the claims of the Fathers' Jewish interlocutors. The arguments in favor of παρθένος employed by Basil in this paragraph are borrowed from Origen, *Against Celsus* 1.34–35; Eusebius of Caesarea, *Demonstration of the Gospel* 7.1, also borrows from Origen.

[47] Is 7.10–12.
[48] Is 7.14.
[49] Is 7.11.
[50] Eph 4.9–10.
[51] Deut 22.28–29.
[52] Mt 1.24.

spouses, having affection for his wife and caring for her in every way. But he abstained from marital relations. For it says: *He did not know her until she had given birth to her firstborn son.*[53] Now this verse has given rise to the conjecture that, after rendering pure service in accomplishing the birth of the Lord through the Holy Spirit, Mary did not renounce the customary marital relations. But in our opinion, even if none of this harms the account of piety—for virginity was necessary for service in the economy,[54] but inquiring into what happened next out of curiosity should be avoided by reason of its mystery—nonetheless, since lovers of Christ do not accept the opinion that the Mother of God[55] ever ceased being a virgin, we think the following testimonies suffice. Let us return to: *He did not know her until she had given birth to her son*. In many instances the word "until" seems to suggest a kind of temporal boundary, but in reality it indicates indefiniteness. What did the Lord mean when he said: *And behold, I am with you all days, until the close of the age*?[56] Indeed, not that the Lord was not going to be with the saints after this age! Rather, it means that the promise of the present age will not be rescinded in the age to come. So we say that in this case too the word "until" should be taken in the same way. Now when *firstborn* is said, by no means is he the firstborn in comparison to siblings who came after him. Rather, he is called the firstborn because he was the first one to open the womb of his mother.[57] It is also clear from the story about Zechariah that Mary was always a virgin. For there is an account, and it has been handed down to us from the tradition, that Zechariah entrusted Mary to the place for the virgins after conceiving the Lord. Then he was slaughtered by the Jews *between the temple and the altar*.[58] Charges

[53]Note that modern critical editions of Mt 1.25 do not include the words 'her firstborn' (αὐτῆς τὸν πρωτότοκον). But there is ample evidence for this reading among mss that display the so-called Byzantine textform, and Basil surely considered these words authentic. Basil's version probably represents a harmonization with Lk 2.7.

[54]Gk. οἰκονομία. See notes 6 and 25 above.

[55]Gk. θεοτόκος, or *Theotokos*.

[56]Mt 28.20.

[57]Cf. Ex 13.2; 13.15; 34.19; Num 3.12.

[58]Mt 23.35.

had been brought against him by the people, on the grounds that by his actions he established that incredible and famous sign: a virgin gave birth and her virginity was not destroyed.[59]

Now when Jesus was born in Bethlehem of Judea in the days of Herod the king, behold, magi from the East came to Jerusalem, saying: "Where is he who has been born the king of the Jews?"[60] The magi are a people of Persia. They are interested in divination, charms, and natural remedies, and devote themselves to the observation of the heavens. It appears that Balaam also practiced this sort of divination. When summoned by Balak to curse Israel using certain words, Balaam in his fourth oracle says the following about the Lord: *A man who sees, who hears the words of God, knows the knowledge of the Most High, and having seen a vision of God in sleep, his eyes were uncovered. I will point to him, but not now; I bless him, but he does not draw near. A star shall arise from Jacob, and a man shall spring out of Israel.*[61] And so, as the magi searched for the place in Judaea mentioned in this ancient prophecy, they came to Jerusalem to learn where the king of the Jews had been born.[62] Perhaps when the Lord's epiphany weakened the power of the adversary at that time, they sensed their own actions becoming ineffectual and attributed great power to the one who had been born. Therefore, when they found the child they adored him with gifts. Even though they are a people alienated from God and a stranger to the covenants, the magi were the first deemed worthy to worship him, since the testimony of enemies is the most credible. Now if the Jews had been the first to worship him, it would have redounded to the glory of their people in the eyes of others. But as it is, they exhibited no interest in worshipping him as God. Hence foreigners worshipped the one whose own people condemned and crucified him.

[59] Here Basil recounts Christian apocryphal traditions found in the *Proto-Gospel of James* 23–24, which he probably found in Origen, *Commentariorum series in evangelium Matthaei* 25 (GCS 38: 42, 14–43, 18 Klostermann-Treu).

[60] Mt 2.1–2. Basil omits the remainder of Mt 2.2, *For we have seen his star in the East, and have come to worship him.*

[61] Num 24.15–17.

[62] See Mt 2.2.

Now since the magi were devoted to the motions of the heavens, they could not ignore it when they beheld something incredible among the heavenly spectacles: a new and unfamiliar star that had risen at the birth of the Lord.

6   No one should draw upon the arguments of astrology to explain the rising of this star. Those who suggest that birth is dependent upon the already existing stars maintain that what happens in each person's life is caused by a particular configuration of the stars. But no configuration of the stars signified the birth of a king in this case, nor was this star one of them. For those stars formed in the beginning along with the rest of creation are either totally motionless or possess unceasing motion. But when this star appeared it seems to have had both, in that it moves and is stationary. Now among the already existing stars, some are fixed and never move, whereas others wander[63] and are never stationary. But since this star both moves and is stationary, it is clear that it belongs to neither category. For it moved from the East to Bethlehem, but it was stationary above that place where the child was. Therefore, when the magi set out from the East, they followed this star as their guide. Upon reaching Jerusalem, their arrival threw the whole city into a tumult, and the magi made the king afraid.[64]

So when the magi found what they had been seeking, they honored him with gifts: gold, frankincense, and myrrh.[65] Perhaps also in giving these gifts they are adhering to the prophecy of Balaam, who spoke of Christ as follows: *Laying down he rested like a lion and like a young lion. Who shall rouse him? Those who bless you are blessed, and those who curse you are cursed.*[66] So then, since Scripture uses the lion to indicate royalty, and laying down to indicate suffering, and the power to bless to indicate divinity, the magi are following the prophecy when they present gold as to a king, frankincense as to one who will die, and myrrh as to God.

[63]Gk. *planētai*, "the wandering stars, or planets."
[64]See Mt 2.3.
[65]See Mt 2.11.
[66]Num 24.9.

Now those whose explanations of issues pertaining to this passage are based on futile investigations cannot claim that this star was similar to comets, which are observed in heaven at a fixed place especially when the successions of kings are revealed. Now on the whole comets are also motionless, since their combustion is confined to a circumscribed place. Comets, whether "beams" or "pits," vary in appearance and the designations given them are based on their appearance.[67] But all of them come into existence in the same way. For when the air surrounding the earth overflows and is diffused into the aethereal region, as it rises there it produces something thick and turbid that is like fuel for a fire and thereby causes a star to appear.[68] Yet when this star appeared in the East, it prompted the magi to seek for the one who had been born. But it did not appear again until it appeared for a second time to the puzzled magi in Judaea, so that they could learn whose star it was, whom it served, and why it had come into being. *For it came to rest over the place where the child was;*[69] hence, *when they saw it they rejoiced with great joy.*[70]

Therefore, let us also welcome this great joy into our hearts. The angels bring good news of this joy to the shepherds.[71] Let us adore with the magi.[72] Let us glorify with the shepherds.[73] Let us sing with the choirs of angels: *For to you is born today a Savior, who is Christ the Lord.*[74] *The Lord is God, and he has shone upon us.*[75] He did not shine upon us in the form of God[76] lest he frighten what is weak; rather, he shone upon us in the form of a slave[77] to free what is enslaved. Who is

[67]Cf. Aristotle, *On the Universe* 4 (395b10–13).

[68]Here Basil summarizes an ancient meteorological theory concerning the formation of stars which has its ultimate origin in Aristotle, *Meteorology* 1.7 (344a4f.)

[69]Mt 2.9.
[70]Mt 2.10.
[71]See Lk 2.10.
[72]See Mt 2.11.
[73]See Lk 2.20.
[74]Lk 2.11.
[75]Ps 118.27 (117.27 LXX).
[76]Cf. Phil 2.6.
[77]Cf. Phil 2.7.

so sluggish of soul, who is so ungrateful, that he does not rejoice and exult and take delight in the present circumstances? It is the feast in which all creation shares. It bestows supercosmic realities upon the world. It sends archangels to Zechariah and to Mary. It forms choirs of angels who sing: *Glory to God in the highest, and on earth peace, good will among men.*[78] The stars run from heaven. The magi move from the nations. The earth provides welcome in a cave. There is no one who has not received some profit, no one who is ungrateful. Let us too raise up the voice of exultation.[79] Let us give our feast a name: the Theophany. Let us celebrate the salvation of the world, the birthday of humanity. Today the condemnation of Adam has been lifted. No longer *are you dust and to dust you shall return;*[80] rather, joined now to heaven, you shall be taken up into heaven. No longer *in pain shall you bring forth children.*[81] For blessed is she who was in travail with Emmanuel, and blessed the breasts which reared him.[82] *For to us a child is born, to us a son is given, and on his shoulders shall be the government.*[83] My heart is alive and well, and my mind is overflowing, but the tongue is deficient and words insufficient to proclaim such great joy.

Please think of the incarnation[84] of the Lord in a way appropriate to God: His divinity is undefiled even though it has come to be in a material nature. It corrects what is subject to passion, but it is not itself filled with passion. Don't you see that this sun[85] has come to be in the mire but is not sullied, that it shines in the filth but does not acquire the stench? On the contrary, it dries up the putrefaction of those with whom it will associate forever.[86] So then, what is it

[78]Lk 2.14. Here Basil is a witness to a common textual variant: εὐδοκία not εὐδοκίας. Textual critics consider the latter the more likely original reading.

[79]Cf. Ps 40.5 (41.5 LXX), 45.2 (46.2 LXX), 118.15 (117.15 LXX).

[80]Gen 3.10.

[81]Gen 3.16.

[82]Cf. Lk 11.27.

[83]Is 9.6.

[84]Gk. ἐνανθρώπησις. See note 29 above.

[85]In this sentence and the next Basil refers to the divinity of Christ metaphorically as the sun.

[86]Namely, the putrefaction of sin.

about his passionless and inviolate nature that makes you fear its wiping away our stains? He was born that you might be cleansed by that which is of the same kind as you.[87] He grew up that you might enter into affinity with him through good habits. O the depth of the goodness of God and his love for humanity! In response to his superabundant gifts we do not put our trust in our Benefactor; in response to the Lord's great love for humanity we rebel against being his servants.[88] O this absurd and wicked ingratitude! The magi adore him but Christians inquire how God can be in flesh, what sort of flesh he has, and whether the humanity he assumed was perfect or imperfect! In the Church of God such superfluous matters should be passed over in silence. Hold in honor what we have long believed. Do not make what has been passed over in silence become the object of pointless speculation. Associate with those who welcome the Lord with joy when he comes from heaven. Think of the shepherds who display their wisdom, the priests who prophesy, the women who are delighted, Mary learning to rejoice from Gabriel, Elizabeth having John leap in her womb.[89] Anna announced good news.[90] Simeon took him in his arms,[91] adoring the great God in a small infant: he did not show contempt for what he saw, but glorified the majesty of his divinity. For the divine power was manifested through the human body, as light through vitreous membranes, and shines upon those who have the eyes of their heart purified. May we also be found among them, *with unveiled face beholding the glory of the Lord,*[92] so that we too may *be transformed from glory to glory,*[93] by the grace of our Lord Jesus Christ and his love for humanity. *To him be glory and might for ever and ever. Amen.*[94]

[87] Gk. συγγενής. See note 16 above.
[88] Cf. *Chr.* 2.
[89] See Lk 1.41.
[90] Cf. Lk 2.36–38.
[91] See Lk 2.28.
[92] 2 Cor 3.18.
[93] Ibid.
[94] As evident in all of the sermons throughout this volume, Basil, like Origen, tends to conclude his homilies with the doxology from 1 Pet 4.11.

On Baptism

1   Solomon the wise said, *All things have their appointed time; there is a time for each event in life: a time to be born and a time to die.*[1] But I would change this wise king's distinction about proper times. In preaching to you of salvation, I would say: There is a time to die and a time to be born. Why this change? Because Solomon referred to the natural order, where birth precedes death (since what has not been born cannot die). But I will be addressing you on a new, spiritual, birth, one where death precedes life. For we are born to the spirit by dying to the flesh. The Lord says, *I bring both death and life.*[2] Let us die, so that we may live. Let us kill our material perspective, which is incapable of submitting to God's law, to give birth to a robust spiritual frame of mind that will open the way to life and peace. Let us be buried with Christ, who died for us, that we may rise with him who is the harbinger of our own resurrection.

Indeed there is a time suitable for all things: a time to sleep, a time to be wakeful, a time for war, a time for peace. But when it comes to baptism, any time is the proper time. The soul must know its creator to live as surely as the body must breathe. For the soul must know God or die. The unbaptized person lacks that inner light, by which the eye can see things properly and the soul can meditate

[1]Eccl 3.1–2. Wherever Basil's biblical citations very closely match the Greek reference texts of late antiquity (the match is often verbatim), the sermons *On Baptism, On Giving Thanks,* and the three sermons on martyrs Julitta, Mamas, and Barlaam, follow the English translation of the New Revised Standard Version. Basil's occasional minor variants (a word substituted or skipped phrase) are reflected in the translation but for the sake of simplicity not indicated in the notes. Readers concerned with the precise biblical terminology in these five translations are encouraged to consult the Greek.

[2]Deut 32.39.

on God. Any time is right for salvation by baptism: whether it is
day, night, a particular hour, or an instant. But the best time is one
that shares the spirit of new birth. What time could be more suitable
than the day of Easter? For that is the day that commemorates the
Resurrection—and it is baptism that facilitates our own resurrection. On the day of Resurrection, therefore, let us receive the grace
of resurrection.

This is why the Church has for so long been calling out, sum-
moning her children from far and wide. Now that she has conceived
and given birth to them, they may, after their nurture on the milk of
catechetical teaching, taste the solid food of doctrine. John preached
a baptism of repentance and everyone in Judaea flocked to hear him.
The Lord proclaims a baptism of adoption; who, hoping in him, will
not obey? John's baptism was merely a beginning; Jesus' baptism is
the perfect consummation. John's baptism made a break from sin;
Jesus' baptism is union with God. John's preaching was the ministry
of one man; it compelled people to repent.

But you postpone the moment. You hesitate and procrastinate
even when you hear the Scriptures that were read in today's lesson:
the Prophet who says, *Be washed, be clean*;[3] the Psalm that admonished you to *Draw near to him and be enlightened*;[4] the Apostle's
amazing promise in the call to *Repent and be baptized, every one, in
the name of Jesus Christ for the remission of sins, and you will receive
the promise of the Holy Spirit*;[5] and the Lord's own invitation, *Come
to me, all you that are weary and are carrying heavy burdens and I
will give you rest*.[6] You have received Christian teaching since your
childhood; do you still hold back from acting on the truth? A lifelong
seeker, will you keep one foot in the door even when you are old and
grey? Will you ever become a Christian? When will we see you as one
of our own? Last year you said you were waiting for this year, and
now you put it off yet another year. Beware lest your promise extend

[3]Is 1.16.
[4]Ps 34.5 (33.6 LXX).
[5]Acts 2.38.
[6]Mt 11.28.

past your allotted time in life. You have no idea what will happen tomorrow; do not make a promise you cannot keep.

We are calling you—yes, you!—to life. Why do you shrug off the invitation? It is an invitation to share in blessings; why disregard such a gift? Heaven's citizenship is open to you, an invitation from the Spirit of truth. The way forward is easy. It requires neither time, nor cost, nor work. Why wait? Why hold back? Why dread the yoke as if you were an ox or steer that had not yet submitted to the master's controlling hand? It is *sweet*; it is *light*.[7] It does not hurt the neck but adorns it. It is not an instrument of bondage, but seeks one who will volunteer to wear it with freedom. Did you notice that Ephraim is charged with wandering about like some goaded heifer, shamefully evading the yoke of the law?[8] Yield that stiff neck of yours. Take on Christ's yoke lest your maverick ways make you easy bait for the wolves in life.

2   *O taste and see that the Lord is good.*[9] How can those who have never tasted it know how honey is sweet? *Taste and see*. Experience makes meaning clear. A Jew does not postpone circumcision, faced with the threat that *every soul who shall not be circumcised on the eighth day shall be utterly destroyed from its family.*[10] But you put off circumcision—not the kind that strips off flesh, but rather baptism. You put it off even after you hear the Lord say, *Very truly I tell you, no one can enter the kingdom of God without being born through*[11] *water and the spirit.*[12] There is pain and a throbbing sore in the first kind of circumcision, but the second provides the dew of heaven and healing for a wounded heart. Do you revere the one who died for you? If so, let yourself be *buried with him through*[13] *baptism.*[14] For unless you

[7]Mt 11.30.
[8]Hos 4.16.
[9]Ps 34.8 (33.9 LXX).
[10]Gen 17.14.
[11]Gk. διά.
[12]Jn 3.5.
[13]Gk. διά.
[14]Col 2.12.

let yourself be sown into the earth together with him in the likeness of his death, how can you be *united with him in resurrection*?[15] Israel was *baptized into Moses in the cloud and in the sea*,[16] providing you with types and an image for truth that would become clear in a later age. But you evade baptism, which is not the symbol typified by the Red Sea crossing, but rather an effective reality; not from the cloud over the Sinai desert sky but through the Spirit; not a baptism into Moses (who was, after all, a servant like yourselves), but into Christ, your creator. The tribe of Israel would not have escaped Pharaoh if it had not gone through the sea. And you—you will certainly not experience liberation from the enemy's terrible power in your life if you do not pass through the water [of baptism]. If Israel had not been baptized—figuratively—it would never have drunk from the spiritual rock. You too, without baptism, can never experience true drink. After his baptism, Israel ate the *bread of angels*;[17] unless you receive baptism, how will you taste the living bread? Through baptism, Israel entered the land of promise; without the seal of baptism, how will you enter paradise? Don't you know that a flaming sword *guards the way of the tree of life*?[18] It is a blade that flickers hot and terrifying to unbelievers; but for believers it radiates with glory and is easy to approach. God causes it to turn, appearing from one perspective to the faithful, but at sword point to those not sealed by baptism.

3   When the chariot of fire and flaming horses approached Elijah, he was not disturbed but in his zeal to ascend he dared to enter the flaming chariot while he was still alive in the flesh.[19] But you face no burning chariot. You can reach heaven through water and the spirit. So why aren't you rushing to answer the call? Elijah demonstrated the power of baptism when he used water instead of fire to consume the sacrifice on the altar. Fire and water work at cross purposes. But

[15]Rom 6.5.
[16]1 Cor 10.2.
[17]Ps 78.25 (77.25 LXX).
[18]Gen 3.24.
[19]2 Kg 2.11.

when the water, a figure of the mystery, was sprinkled three times on the altar, it flamed up as if fed by oil: *"Fill buckets with water,"* he said, *"and pour it upon the burnt offering and on the wood." And he said, "Do it a second time." And they did it a second time. Again he said, "Do it a third time." And they did it a third time.*[20] The Word here shows that the one who comes to God through baptism is affiliated with God. By their faith in the Trinity, a pure and heavenly light illuminates those who approach by baptism.

If I were giving out gold to those assembled here, you would hardly tell me, "I will come tomorrow and you can give it to me then." Rather, you would push your way forward now to receive your share, resisting any delay. But offered the greatest gift—purity for your soul and not some gaudy substance—you create excuses and list reasons for delay, instead of hurrying up for your share. And what a marvelous gift it is: that you might be renewed without going through destruction, formed anew without first coming apart, healed without suffering! But the gift means little to you.

If you were a slave and there were an announcement offering manumission, wouldn't you hurry to the appointed time, hiring lawyers, begging the judges to grant you freedom, doing whatever was necessary? Indeed, you would likely tolerate even that one last slap every slave receives at being freed, since it means entering into freedom and immunity. But now the divine messenger calls you—a slave to sin rather than to another human being—to grant you citizenship equal to the angels, to make you a free child of God through adoption, heir to Christ's blessings. And you say you are not ready!

What abysmal excuses! Delayed by dishonorable and perpetual distractions! How long will you run after pleasure? We have given the world so much of our lives; let us protect what is left to us, to use for our true benefit. What value compares with the soul? What equals the kingdom of heaven? What advisor is more trustworthy than Christ? Who is more prudent than the wise? More useful than he who is good? Who is closer to us than the creator? We would

[20] 1 Kg 18.33–34.

hardly say that Eve benefited from following the serpent's advice instead of the Lord's. What stupid claims you make, insisting, "I do not have time for healing. Do not show me the light just yet. I'm not quite ready to unite with the King." Do you deny making such extreme assertions? But indeed you do, and you say other things that are even more foolish.

If you were a debtor burdened with public liability and there were a debt relief option, you would object loudly if anyone tried to prevent you from taking advantage of this generosity. But you cause harm to yourself that is worse even than those inflicted by an enemy in the face of this opportunity for not only past but also future immunity. Surely you do not really believe that you have made the right choice—that it is wise to hold back from such a gift, to be excluded eternally? After all, we know that even the slave who owed ten thousand talents would have experienced forgiveness of his entire debt if he had not, by abusing his fellow slave, perpetuated his debt to his master.[21] Let us beware lest this happen to us also, that after we have obtained grace we lose it again by refusing to forgive our debtors.

4 Look inward, to the secret depths of your own soul. Take inventory of your conscience. Do not despair if you find you have many sins, for *where sin increased, grace abounded all the more*,[22] if, that is, you receive grace. Much is forgiven the one who owes much—so he might love more. But if, on the other hand, you hesitate over baptism even though your debt from past sins is small and *not mortal*,[23] then why are you so worried about [what you might do that could dishonor your baptism in] the future, especially if your past is not dishonorable and you simply lacked proper instruction?[24] Imagine

[21]Mt 18.24–35.

[22]Rom 5.20.

[23]1 Jn 5.17.

[24]Cyprian of Carthage also stressed that forgiveness would continue to be available through penance after baptism, since, without it, "who would not fall away in utter despair, who would not give up any thought of sorrowing for sin?" *Letter* 55.28.1, trans. G.W. Clarke, *The Letters of St. Cyprian of Carthage* (New York: Newman Press, 1986), vol. 3, 51.

your soul in a balance, devils and angels pulling at it in different directions. Which side will your heart defend? Who will win you over? Will it be fleshly delights or the holy soul? Present pleasure or a longing for the world to come? Will angels welcome you or will what you are tightly grasping now continue to own you?

Commanders on the battlefield provide their soldiers with a password or token to equip them to call for help readily and to recognize one another clearly in any combat. But no one will recognize you, as belonging to either us or the enemy, if you fail to display the proper secret signs. How can the angel confirm your identity if you are not marked with the light of the Lord's countenance?[25] How can he rescue you from the foe if he sees no sign of your allegiance? Don't you recall that the Angel of Death spared homes that had the mark, but killed the firstborn in homes without it?[26] Unidentified riches are most liable to theft. Sheep are easy to steal if they have not been branded.

5   Are you still a youth? Apply the reins of baptism to be master over your youth. Has your flower faded? Do not lose what you still have. Do not waste your resources, or think the eleventh hour is really only the first. And the one enjoying the first hour should be mindful of the final hour. If a physician promised that he would rejuvenate you, using his skills and efforts to restore your past youthfulness, wouldn't you be restless, impatiently waiting for the promised day? But now, promised baptism with its rejuvenation of your old sin-deformed soul to a fresh splendor, you scorn the benefactor, and stand unmoved. Don't you want to experience the promised miraculous transformation? How does one experience new birth without a mother? How does one restore to the bloom of youth the old self, corrupted and deluded by its lusts?[27]

Baptism: This is what buys back captives, forgives debts, and indelibly marks its recipients. It is the heavenly chariot, the sure

[25]Ps 4.6.
[26]Ex 12.23.
[27]Eph 4.22.

promise of the kingdom, the grace of adoption. Do you really think, wretch, that pleasure is better than such blessed benefits?

I see your delay even when you try to conceal it. Even if you are silent, your action speaks louder than your words. It says: "Just let me use the body for shameful pleasure; I want to wallow in this delightful muck. I will get blood on my hands; I will rob from others; I will behave deceitfully; I will curse and lie. And when I stop sinning, then I will get baptized."

Keep it up, if sin is good. But if sin can hurt the sinner, why do you persist in doing yourself damage? No one continues to eat what is harmful and excessive if they are trying to clear the body of bile. It would be better to purge the body of what ails it, not provoke an intolerable sickness. A ship stays afloat as long as it can hold up under the ballast of what it carries, but if it takes on too much cargo, it sinks. You ought indeed to worry that this might happen to you—that the weight of your sins may shipwreck you before you reach your goal. Does God not see all? Doesn't he know your inner thoughts? Do you think he is collaborating in all those things you are doing wrong? *You thought*, he says, *that I was one just like yourself.*[28]

Whenever you want to make friends with someone, you win the person over with acts of kindness, saying and doing what you think they will like. But when you want a close relationship with God and hope even for adoption into the family, do you really think the best behavior is to offend him? Will you become God's close friend by violating his law? In your hope for liberation, watch out that you are not stockpiling things so toxic with all your sins that you will lose hope of pardon; *God is not mocked.*[29] Beware of gambling with grace. Do not say, "Yes, the law is good, but sin is so much more fun." Pleasure is the devil's hook, baiting us toward destruction. Pleasure is the mother of sin, and *the wages of sin is death.*[30] Pleasure feeds the worm that is always tickling us; it gives a moment of delight but

[28]Ps 50.21 (49.21 LXX).
[29]Gal 6.7.
[30]1 Cor 15.56.

then spasms of disgust. Nothing puts off the goal more effectively than the idea, "Let sin have its rule first, then the Lord can take over. I will let my body be *an instrument of unrighteousness for the sake of lawlessness*, and then I will afterwards present my members to God as *instruments of righteousness*."[31] This is just what Cain did with his sacrifices: the first portion for his own use, and a second-quality cut of the goods for God, his creator and benefactor. While you have your strength, you waste your best energies on what is sinful. Only when you lose your strength do you plan to devote your body to God, when it is feeble with age and good for nothing else. Such "self-control" in old age is just another word for impotence! No one puts a crown on a corpse. The inability to do evil is not in itself justice. Use your reason to take control over sin while you still can. This is virtue: *Turn away from evil and do good*.[32] There is nothing to praise or condemn if evil is simply not taking place. If your old age limits you from sinful behavior, this is nothing more than the benefit of incapacity. We praise those who actively choose virtue, not those who are forced into it by their physical deficiencies.

What is the assigned limit of your life? Who guarantees that you will live to old age? Who can be so sure of the future? Don't you see infants who die suddenly, and adults who succumb at the height of their best years? Life has no fixed term for everyone. So why do you wait for that fatal fever as the time to be baptized? You may find yourself unable to speak for salvation. The disease in your head may block your ears. You will be able neither to lift your hands to heaven, stand upright, give proper bodily worship for the ritual, learn properly, confess clearly, join with God, nor renounce the devil. Most likely you would not even be capable of attending to the service, and those around you may doubt whether you even perceive grace or perhaps remain unconscious. But even if you do clearly know what is taking place, you will have the prize without the profit.

[31]Rom 6.13.
[32]1 Pet 3.11.

6   Follow the example of the eunuch.[33] He found a teacher and paid attention to his instruction. Although the eunuch was rich, he invited the poor man to join him on his chariot. Although he was a man with power and influence, he invited up someone lowly and common. He did not delay the Spirit's seal when he learned of the gospel of the kingdom, and accepted it wholeheartedly. Indeed, when they came near some water, he said, *Look, here is water!* He spoke with joy, and said, *What hinders me from being baptized?*[34] When the will is ready, nothing can stand in the way. For the one who calls loves mankind; the deacon is prepared; grace is plentiful; all is ardent longing; there are no hindrances whatsoever.

Facing us is only one hindrance: the one who creates a roadblock between ourselves and salvation. We can conquer him, if we are prudent. He suggests that we put baptism off for another time; let us respond by standing up to act. He tricks our heart with empty promises; let us be alert to his wiles. Is it not this enemy who suggests that we sin today, and wait until tomorrow to be good? This is why the Lord, opposed to such perversity, says: *O that today you would listen to my voice.*[35] That one says, "Today for me; tomorrow for God." But the Lord answers, *Listen to my voice today.*

Take note of the enemy's method. He does not dare to suggest that you abandon God utterly (for he knows that even Christian catechumens would be shocked to hear this). Rather, he uses fraud to attack indirectly. He is *wise in doing evil.*[36] He knows that we live for the moment, and that everything we do is in the present tense. Skillfully, then, he robs us of today and leaves us with nothing but hope for tomorrow. But when tomorrow comes, back he trots, commanding this new day as well, and once again suggests "tomorrow for the Lord." Using pleasure as his bait, he repeats this tactic day after day. We are left hoping for the future, while he robs us of our very life.

[33]Acts 8.27–39.
[34]Acts 8.36.
[35]Ps 95.7 (94.8 LXX).
[36]Jer 4.22.

7   I once watched a mother bird perform a similar trick. She fluttered around the hunters in order to divert their attention from her chicks, vulnerable in their nest. She made sure she would not be caught, but she kept on teasing the hunters with hope. After in various ways deluding their expectations, keeping their focus on her diversion, she gave the chicks time to take wing, and then they all flew off together.

Beware lest you be tricked in the same manner, gambling your one opportunity for present good with evasive hopes. Come to me this very instant. Hand yourself over wholeheartedly to the Lord. Put your name on the list. Be enrolled in the church. A soldier is enlisted in the armed forces. An athlete enters his name in to be counted in the competition. A naturalized citizen is registered in the city records. You are all of these things to God: a soldier of Christ, an athlete competing in piety, and one whose citizenship belongs in heaven. Have your name recorded in this book so that it will be on record above. Take instruction; learn the gospel rules of the land. They include discipline of the eyes; government over the tongue; proper service of the body; humility of mind; pure thinking; turning away from anger; going beyond that which is expected of you; not taking others to court over what they have stolen; responding to hatred with love; enduring persecution; and when insulted, appealing to harmony. Be dead to sin. Be crucified with Christ, your whole heart in love with the Lord.

Yes these are hard things to put into practice. But what good thing is ever easy? Who ever lifted the winning cup while they were asleep? Who was ever crowned for valor while indulging in a soft life and enjoying the music? No one can win the prize for a race without running. Hard work merits glory; you do need to fight to get the crown; *Through tribulations we must enter the kingdom of heaven.*[37] And while I fully agree with this saying, it is also true that the blessings of the heavenly kingdom release us from these tribulations, while the anguish and sorrow of hell stalk the activities of sin.

[37] Acts 14.21.

If you think about it, you will see that not even the works of the devil are effortless for sinners. How much does continence make us perspire? But debauchery is exhausting. Does moderation take as much out of us as shameful frenetic passion? Indeed it is true that those who commit themselves to prayer vigil go nights without sleeping. But those spent in being naughty are much more difficult, since the fear of being discovered and the nervous energy of hedonism destroys all sense of rest. If you continue to run away from the narrow road to salvation, following sin's path instead to its logical conclusion, I fear you will indeed come to what is at its end.

But such treasure, you say, is hard to protect. Work at it, brother! Use those who are given to you to be assistants: prayer as a night watchman, fasting as the servant at the door, psalmody as your soul-guide. Take them along; they will keep watch with you to guard your priceless treasure. Which is better: to be rich and expend some effort to insure the security of your wealth? Or to have nothing that is worth protecting? No one abandons his goods simply because he is afraid to lose them. If that were the case, no one would ever try for anything at all. Farming is liable to the risk of crop failure; shipwreck threatens commerce; those who marry are widowed; children's education is endangered by the loss of their parents. And yet we engage in these activities, encouraged by hope, trusting the outcome to God, who orders all things. You give lip service to sanctity, while your deeds place you firmly among those who are condemned. See that you do not find it too late when you make up your mind to repent!

Consider the foolish virgins.[38] Not having oil in their lamps, they noticed that they were short just when it was time to go in and join the wedding party. Thus the Scripture calls them foolish. They spent time searching for oil just when they should have been enjoying the outcome of their efforts, and as a result lost their chance of joining the wedding feast. Watch out, lest you too arrive at that unexpected day when your resources run out because you have procrastinated, year by year, month by month, day by day, the simple act of taking

[38]Mt 25.1–12.

enough oil to nourish your enlightenment. Everything around you will come up short on that day: inconsolable afflictions, no hope from the physicians, and those of your own house will be powerless to help. With dry gasping, short of breath, consumed by a burning fever, you will moan from the heart but without winning any sympathy. You will say something so faint and indistinct that no one will hear you, or will think you are simply muttering mindlessly. Who will give you baptism then? Who will remind you when you are barely conscious? Those nearby will be disheartened. Outsiders will not care. A friend will not want to remind you for fear it will add further stress. Possibly even the physician will hold out on you. You yourself, with a natural love for life, may not admit the truth. And then the night will come, and all desert you. There is no one to give you baptism. Death itself stands beside you, its attendants at hand to carry you off. Who will rescue you? Will God, whom you have scorned? But he will listen to you then, perhaps—if you will listen to him now. Will he give you a second chance? So well have you used what you were given!

8   *Do not be led astray by vain words.*[39] For *sudden destruction*[40] will strike like a storm. The Angel of Darkness will arrive and forcefully drag away your sin-bound soul. The soul will lament in vain, its body no longer responding to its distress. O, how you will want to tear yourself apart with anguish! How you will sigh! Then you will repent in vain for all that you failed to do when you were licking your lips to follow those evil whisperings. You will witness both the joy of the righteous ones, glorified by their heavenly rewards, and sinners lamenting in deepest darkness. What will you say then, in your heartfelt anguish? "Woe is me, that I did not heave off this heavy load of sin when I had the chance! Now I have pulled it down on myself, for my own destruction! Woe is me, that I did not wash away my stains, but remain stinking with sin! I would have been with God's

[39]Eph 5.6.
[40]1 Thess 5.3.

angels now, enjoying the good things of heaven. Oh, what wrong choices I made! For time-bound pleasures I now face eternal torment. Because of fleshly hedonism, I am delivered into the fire. God's judgment is just: I was called and I did not obey. I was taught, and did not learn. They told me this would happen, but I laughed it off."

With these words and others like them you will cry out against what is happening if you are taken away unbaptized. Fear hell, man, or at least make an effort to gain the kingdom. Do not ignore the summons. Do not grasp at this or that reason to say, "Hold me excused." There is no reason at all for excuse. I am impelled to tears, deeply troubled, that you prefer shameful shenanigans instead of the great glory of God. You shortchange yourself of promised blessings by holding onto sin and do not see the good things of the heavenly Jerusalem: thousands of angels, the festival of the first-born, the thrones of the apostles, the honored seats of the prophets, scepters of patriarchs, crowns of martyrs, and the choral fellowship[41] of the righteous. Set your heart on being added to this list, washed and sanctified by the gift of Christ, to whom be glory and might, forever and ever. Amen.

---

[41]Or, "choirs."

First Homily on Fasting

1 *Blow the trumpet at the new moon, on the glorious day of your feast.*[1] This is the Prophet's command. But the readings suggest to us a feast that surpasses the one celebrated in those days, more resounding than every trumpet and more glorious than every musical instrument. For Isaiah has taught us the grace of fasting, rejecting the Jewish manner of fasting and showing us the true fast. *Do not fast to quarrel and fight, but loose every bond of iniquity.*[2] And the Lord [adds]: *Do not be gloomy, but wash your face and anoint your head.*[3] So let us acquire the disposition that we have been taught, not looking gloomy on the days [of fasting] we are currently observing, but cheerfully disposed toward them, as is fitting for the saints. No one crowned is despondent; no one glum holds up a trophy. Do not be gloomy while you are being healed. It is absurd not to rejoice in the soul's health, and rather to sorrow over the change in food and to appear to favor the pleasure of the stomach over the care of the soul. After all, while self-indulgence gratifies the stomach, fasting brings gain to the soul. Be cheerful since the physician has given you sin-destroying medicine. For just as worms breeding in the intestines of children are utterly eradicated by the most pungent medicines, so too, when a fast truly worthy of this designation is introduced into the soul, it kills the sin that lurks deep within.

2 *Anoint your head and wash your face.*[4] The word invites you to mysteries. He who "anoints" himself applies oil [to his bodily

[1] Ps 81.3 (80.4 LXX).
[2] Is 58.4, 6.
[3] Mt 6.16–17.
[4] Mt 6.17.

members], and he who "washes" himself cleanses himself. Take this prescription as referring to your interior members. Cleanse your soul of sin, and apply holy chrism to your head, that you may share in Christ.[5] And so, approach the fast in this way. Do not disfigure your face like the hypocrites.[6] You disfigure your face[7] when your interior disposition is concealed by a sham external appearance, hidden by a lie as if covered under a veil. He is a hypocrite who assumes in the theater an identity[8] that is not his own. Though a slave, he often assumes the identity of a master; though a private citizen, that of the emperor. Similarly, in this life many act as if they were playing themselves on a stage, carrying in their heart one thing but superficially displaying something else to people. So then, do not disfigure your face. Appear such as you are. Do not doll yourself up with gloom in an attempt to win renown by the appearance of self-control. After all, good deeds when trumpeted bring no benefit and fasting when publicized brings no gain. Ostentatious deeds do not bear fruit that extends to the age to come but culminate in being praised by others.

Therefore run cheerfully to the gift of fasting. Fasting is an ancient gift, not one antiquated and obsolete, but ever fresh and at the height of its vitality.

3 Do you think that I posit the antiquity of fasting on the basis of the law? Indeed, fasting is older than the law. If you were to stay a bit longer, you will discover the truth of my statement. Do not suppose that the Day of Atonement (which for Israel was assigned to the seventh month, on the tenth day of the month)[9] was the beginning of fasting. Come then, let us go through the historical narrative and investigate the antiquity of fasting. For it is not a recent discovery;

[5]Basil's wordplay here is untranslatable: "apply (*chrisai*) holy chrism (*chrisma*) to your head, that you may share in Christ (*Christos*)."

[6]See Mt 6.16.

[7]Gk. πρόσωπον.

[8]Gk. πρόσωπον.

[9]See Lev 25.9.

it is the treasure stored up by our ancestors. Everything that can be traced back to ancient times is venerable. Revere the antiquity of fasting!

Fasting is as old as humanity: it was legislated in paradise. It was the first command that Adam received: *You shall not eat from the tree of the knowledge of good and evil.*[10] *You shall not eat* legislates fasting and self-control. If Eve had fasted from the tree, we would not need this fasting now. *For those who are well have no need of a physician, but those who are sick.*[11] We have been injured by sin; let us be healed by repentance. But repentance is futile without fasting. *Cursed is the ground; thorns and thistles it shall bring forth to you.*[12] You have been ordered to be sorrowful, not to indulge yourself.[13] Make satisfaction to God through fasting. Now the manner of life in paradise is an image of fasting, not only insofar as man, sharing the life of the angels, achieved likeness to them by being content with little, but also because those who lived in paradise had still not dreamt up what humans later discovered through their inventiveness:[14] there was still no drinking of wine, still no animal sacrifices, not to mention whatever else beclouds the human mind.

4 It is because we did not fast that we were banished from paradise. So let us fast that we may return to it.[15] Don't you realize that Lazarus

[10]Gen 2.17.

[11]Mt 9.12.

[12]Gen 3.17–18.

[13]Augustine quotes "it was legislated in paradise ... not to indulge yourself" as testimony for the doctrine of original sin, noting specifically that these lines are from Basil's sermon *On Fasting*, in his *Contra Iulianum* 1.5.18 (PL 44.652). Augustine alludes to the same passage in 1.7.32 (PL 44.663): "Saint Basil tells you that you have sustained the injury of sin because Eve chose not to fast from the forbidden tree" (*Dicit tibi sanctus Basilius, nos aegritudinem contraxisse peccati, quoniam Eva noluit a ligno prohibito ieiunare*).

[14]Gk. ἐπίνοια.

[15]Augustine twice quotes the first two lines of this section as testimony for the doctrine of original sin, each time noting specifically that they are from Basil's sermon *On Fasting*, in his *Contra Iulianum opus imperfectum* 1.52 (CSEL 85/1: 47 Zelzer) and *Contra Iulianum* 5.18 (PL 44.652). Augustine alludes to the same passage in 1.7.32 (PL

entered paradise through fasting?[16] Do not imitate the disobedience of Eve. Then again, do not take the serpent as your advisor, who suggests that you eat out of regard for the flesh. Do not use bodily weakness and illness as an excuse. For you are not giving such excuses to me but to someone who already knows.[17] Tell me, are you unable to fast? Are you able to stuff yourself throughout life? Are you able to wreck your body with the heaviness of the food you've eaten? And yet I know that physicians do not prescribe a variety of foods for the sick, but rather not eating and going without food. So then, if you are able to comply with one [treatment], how can you allege that you cannot follow the other? What is easier for the stomach? To pass the night with plain fare? Or for it to lie there weighed down by an abundance of food? Or rather, not for it to lie there, but for it to be constantly upset, bloated, and grumbling?

Indeed, you wouldn't claim that it is easier for pilots to save a cargo ship loaded down with goods than one less laden and lighter, would you? After all, a slight swelling of the waves has sunk the heavily weighted cargo ship, whereas one that has a moderate amount of freight easily rises above the waves, since nothing hinders it from floating above them. And so, when human bodies are weighed down with unremitting self-indulgence, they are easily inundated with illnesses. But when bodies take nourishment that is light and easy, they escape the impending evil that arises from sickness like a swelling storm, and they evade the present distress that acts like the assault of a tempest. Surely you must think that keeping still is more strenuous than running, and resting more strenuous than wrestling, if indeed you really claim that self-indulgence is more appropriate for the sick

44.663): "Finally he [Basil] says that we have been banished from paradise because we did not fast, and so that we may return to it he orders that we fast" (*Dicit postremo, nos de paradiso decidisse, quia non ieiunavimus, atque ut illo redeamus, praecipit ieiunemus*).

[16]See Lk 16.20–31.

[17]Gk. τῷ εἰδότι λέγεις. Ducaeus identifies this as a proverb (PG 31.1795); see e.g. Pseudo-Plato, *Greater Hippias* 301d. His reference to Cicero's letters to Atticus (9.7.3) should be ignored, resting as it does on the old edition of Erasmus.

than eating lightly. In fact, the faculty that keeps the body alive easily digests a moderate amount of light food and makes it suitable for nourishment. But upon receiving a variety of extravagant foods and then not being satisfied with reaching its limit, it engenders many kinds of sickness.

5   But our homily should be proceeding through the historical narrative, discussing in detail the antiquity of fasting. All the saints received fasting as a kind of paternal inheritance, observed it as such, and handed it on, father to child. And so, through a chain of succession, this asset has been preserved even for us. In paradise there was no wine; there were still no animal sacrifices, still no eating of meat. After the flood: wine; after the flood: [God said] *eat everything, as you eat green plants.*[18] The enjoyment of meat was conceded only when the hope of perfection was lost.

But it is Noah who provides proof that there was no experience of wine, for he did not know how to consume it. After all, the consumption of wine had still not been introduced to the human lifestyle, nor had it become the custom of people. So then, because Noah had neither seen another consuming wine, nor experienced it himself, he drank of it without due precaution and succumbed to the harm it inflicted. For *Noah planted a vineyard, and drank of the wine, and became drunk*[19]—not because he was a drunkard, but because he did not know how to partake of it moderately. And so, the invention of drinking wine is more recent than paradise, and thus the dignity of fasting is ancient.

Yet we also know that Moses arrived at the mountain through fasting.[20] For when the peak was covered with smoke, he would have neither dared nor had the confidence to enter into the thick darkness unless he had armed himself with fasting. Through fasting he received the law written on the tablets by the finger of God.[21]

[18]Gen 9.3.
[19]Gen 9.20–21.
[20]See Ex 24.18.
[21]See Ex 31.18; Deut 9.10.

Furthermore, on the heights, fasting facilitated the delivery of the law, whereas in the valley below gluttony drove the people into the madness of idolatry. For *the people sat down to eat and drink, and rose up to play.*[22] The diligence of the worshipper who fasted and prayed for forty days[23] was rendered useless by a single instance of drunkenness. For while fasting obtained the tablets written by the finger of God,[24] drunkenness shattered them. The Prophet judged the drunken people unworthy to receive the law from God. In one decisive moment, through gluttony, that people who had been taught about God by the greatest marvels plunged themselves into the idolatry of the Egyptians.[25] Compare these two: see how fasting conveys to God and how self-indulgence forsakes salvation.[26] That people descended, proceeding along the way to the world below.

6   What defiled Esau and made him the servant of his brother?[27] Wasn't it a single meal, for the sake of which he forsook his birthright?[28] Wasn't Samuel granted to his mother when she joined fasting to her prayer?[29] What made the great hero Samson unconquerable? Wasn't it fasting? Wasn't it with the aid of fasting that he was conceived in the womb of his mother?[30] Fasting caused him to grow within her womb. Fasting nursed him. Fasting raised him to manhood. It was fasting that the angel had prescribed to his mother: *She may not eat anything that comes from the vine, nor may she drink wine or strong drink.*[31]

[22] Ex 32.6.
[23] See Ex 24.18.
[24] See Ex 31.18; Deut 9.10.
[25] See Ex 32.1–35.
[26] Gk. προδίδωσι. Colbertinus codex primus reads: "chases away" (ἀποδιώκει). Garnier calls it "a reading not to be despised" (*non contemnenda lectio*). PG 31.171 n. 21.
[27] Ms Colbertinus primus reads: "made him the servant *for* his brother."
[28] See Gen 25.30–34.
[29] See 1 Sam 1.13–16.
[30] See Judg 13.4.
[31] Jude 13.14.

Fasting begets prophets and strengthens mighty men. Fasting makes lawgivers wise. It is a good guardian of the soul, a safe companion for the body, the best weapon, a training regimen for contestants. It drives away temptations. It readies[32] for piety. It is the companion of sobriety and the craftsman of self-control. In war it teaches bravery, in peace stillness. It sanctifies the Nazirite[33] and perfects the priest. For it is impossible to venture upon priestly activities without fasting, not only in the case of our present holy and true worship, but also in the prefigured worship set out in the law.

By fasting, Elijah became a spectator of a great spectacle.[34] For after he purified his soul through a forty-day fast, he was deemed worthy of seeing the Lord in the cave on Horeb, insofar as it is possible for a human being to see the Lord.[35] While fasting, he restored the child to the widow, fasting granting him power over death.[36] When the people transgressed the law, the voice sounding from the mouth of the one who was fasting shut the heavens for three years and six months.[37] That he might tame the wild heart of that stiff-necked people, he chose to condemn himself along with others in that catastrophe. Hence: *As the Lord lives, there shall not be water upon the earth, except by my mouth.*[38] And he introduced all the people to fasting through famine in order to correct the wickedness that comes from self-indulgence and a dissolute life.

What sort of life did Elisha have? How did he enjoy the Shunammite's hospitality?[39] How did he receive the prophets? Didn't wild

---

[32]Gk. ἀλείθει, lit. "anoints the skin with oil." Athletes received such an anointing in preparation for competitions.

[33]Garnier notes a marginal gloss on this word in Colbertinus codex primus: τὸν μοναχόν, "the monk."

[34]Gk. θεάματος, "spectacle." Garnier notes ample ms support for θαύματος, "wonder, miracle," and one could plausibly choose either reading.

[35]See 1 Kg 19.8–13.

[36]See 1 Kg 17.17–24.

[37]See 1 Kg 17.1–7; Lk 4.25; Jas 5.17.

[38]1 Kg 17.1. I have omitted the word ἔφη, "he said," after "As the Lord lives" because Garnier notes that it is absent from the mss Garnier seems to have included it because previous editions had.

[39]See 2 Kg 4.8–37.

vegetables and a little bit of meal fulfill the obligations of hospitality? When the gourd had been added to the pot and the men who tasted it were on the verge of danger, the poison was neutralized only by the prayer of the one fasting.[40] And in general you will find that fasting guided all the saints to a godly way of life.

There is a certain corporeal substance called *amianton* or "indestructible" that is impregnable to fire.[41] When placed in flames, it appears to burn to cinders. But when removed from the fire, it turns out to be purer than before, as if polished by water. The three young men in Babylon had such bodies, having acquired their indestructibility[42] through fasting.[43] When they were in the great fiery furnace, as if having the nature of gold, they showed that they were impervious to any harm that the fire could cause.[44] Indeed, they showed that they were even more powerful than gold since the fire did not melt them but rather kept them intact. In fact, nothing at that time could have checked those flames. Naphtha and pitch and brush stoked that fire, so much so that it reached a height of forty-nine cubits and destroyed many Chaldaeans when it leapt out of the furnace.[45] And so, entering with fasting, the young men trounced that conflagration, breathing light and dewy air in the midst of such a furious fire.[46] In fact, the fire did not even dare to singe their hair, since it too had been nourished by fasting.[47]

[40]See 2 Kg 4.38–41.

[41]Gk. ἀμίαντον, which means literally "undefiled." Here Basil refers an asbestos-like mineral used for a variety of purposes in antiquity. The first-century CE Pedanius Dioscorides of Cilician Anazarbus wrote (*De materia medica* 5.138): "Amianton rock is produced in Cyprus, being suitable as fine astringent. Since it is fibrous, the men there weave it into robes for the theater. It burns when thrown in fire, but emerges brighter and completely unconsumed." Pliny the Elder wrote (*Natural History* 36.139): "Amianton like alum loses nothing to fire. It is resistant to all poisons, especially those of sorcerers."

[42]Gk. τὸ ἀμίαντον.
[43]See Dan 1.8–16; 3.19–97 LXX.
[44]See Dan 3.94 LXX.
[45]See Dan 3.46–48.
[46]See Dan 3.49–50.
[47]See Dan 3.94 LXX.

7   Daniel, *the man of desires*,[48] neither ate bread nor drank water for three weeks.[49] And he taught the lions to fast when he climbed down into their den.[50] For just as lions cannot sink their teeth into anything constructed of stone or metal or any other solid material, so too fasting, by hardening the body of that man as tempering hardens iron, made it as hard as steel to the lions. For they did not open their mouth against the saint. Fasting quenched the power of fire and kept away the mouths of the lions.

Fasting sends prayer up to heaven, as if it were its wings for the upward journey. Fasting is the expansion of households, the mother of health, the pedagogue of youth, an adornment for seniors, a good companion on journeys, and a safe housemate for married couples. A husband does not suspect treachery in his marriage when he observes his wife living with fasting. Nor is a wife consumed with jealousy when she observes her husband embracing fasting. Who has suffered the loss of his household possessions when fasting? Count what's in your house today, and count it after the fast. Nothing will be missing from your household possessions because of fasting.

[48]Dan 10.11 θ.

[49]See Dan 10.2–3, which reads: "I ate no desirable bread, no meat or wine (οἶνος) entered my mouth, nor did I anoint myself with oil until I fulfilled three weeks." The discord between the scriptural text, which mentions "wine" (οἶνος) and Basil's statement, which mentions "water" (ὕδωρ), is problematic. In a note (PG 31, 173 n. 31) Garnier takes previous translators to task for their solutions. He accuses Erasmus of dereliction of duty as a translator (*interpretis neglecto munere*) for rendering the phrase καὶ ὕδωρ μὴ πιών ("nor drank water") as *nec vinum bibisset* ("nor drank wine") and concludes: "here, as is often the case elsewhere, the man who is otherwise so erudite is guilty of excessive indulgence." Ducaeus had offered another solution, identifying the scriptural reference as Dan 1.12, which describes the diet of Daniel and the three other young men who were captives in Babylon: "Let us be given vegetables to eat and water to drink." Garnier notes: "But the man who is so learned does not help Basil at all. For he does not vindicate him from the error, but exchanges one error for another. For it is well understood from these words of Daniel that Daniel and the other captive young men drank. Therefore, if Basil was thinking about the daily diet of the captive young men, how could he have written that Daniel did *not* drink water?" Garnier's solution is to maintain that Basil refers to Dan 10.2–3, but "that he suffered a memory lapse, which sometimes happens even to the best of men, and carelessly wrote ὕδωρ ('water') instead of οἶνος ('wine')."

[50]Cf. Dan 6.17–25.

No animal bemoans death: an implacable stomach neither sheds the blood of animals nor issues an order for their slaughter. The butcher puts down his knife and the table is content with plants.

The Sabbath was given to the Jews, it says, that *your donkey and your manservant* might rest.[51] Let fasting be for your household servants a rest from their perpetual labors, seeing that they serve you for the whole year. Give your meat cook a rest. Give your tablesetter a holiday. Stay the hand of your winepourer. Give some time off to your pastry chef, who makes a variety of desserts. Give your household some quiet from the endless clamor, from the smoke and cooking aromas, and from the servants who run up and down to cater to your stomach as if it were an imperious lady. As a matter of fact, even tax collectors permit their subordinates a little freedom. Your stomach should also give your mouth a kind of vacation and agree to a five-day truce with us,[52] seeing that it makes endless demands but never ceases, forgetting tomorrow what it received today. When it's full, it philosophizes about self-control; when it's empty, it forgets these teachings.

8 Fasting knows nothing of the practice of money lending.[53] The table of the one fasting does not reek of interest earned. Inherited debt does not squeeze the faster's orphaned child like a serpent wrapping itself around its prey. In addition, fasting is an opportunity for good cheer. After all, just as thirst makes drinking pleasurable and hunger before a meal makes eating it pleasurable, so too fasting enhances the enjoyment of food when it is partaken. For when

---

[51] Ex 20.10.

[52] Here Basil alludes to the fact that he and his congregation are on the verge of a five-day fast (see also §10 below, as well as *Second Homily on Fasting* chapters four and seven). It is possible that Basil refers to one of the five-day periods of fasting (Monday through Friday) observed during a Lent of seven or eight weeks, a practice known in early Christianity; on this interpretation, Saturday and Sunday would not be fast days during Lent. Another interpretation is that this homily was preached immediately before the Paschal fast, which was observed during Holy Week. In most places, however, the Paschal fast lasted six days, from Monday to Saturday of Holy Week. Yet is unclear why a Paschal fast of only five days might have been practiced in Cappadocia in Basil's era.

[53] Gk. δανείου φύσιν.

fasting has interposed itself as a moderator and interrupted your continual self-indulgence, it will show you that eating is desired so long as it is postponed. Accordingly, if you wish to prepare yourself a table that arouses desire, accept the change introduced by fasting. But because you are overly attached to self-indulgence, you have failed to notice that you make self-indulgence banal to yourself and destroy its pleasure by love of pleasure. For while there is nothing so desirable that it does not become loathsome through continual enjoyment, what is taken rarely is enjoyed quite eagerly. Thus he who created us has made the grace of his gifts endure amidst the changes of this life. Don't you realize that the sun is more enjoyable after the night? That waking is more pleasurable after sleep? That health is more appreciated after the experience of the contrary? So too is the table more charming after fasting: this diet is equally valid for the rich with a sumptuous spread as it is for the poor who eat whatever is near at hand.

9   The example of the rich man should make you afraid.[54] His lifelong self-indulgence brought him to the fire. For he was broiled in the flames of the furnace not on the charge of wickedness but of living sumptuously. We need water to extinguish that fire. Fasting is not only beneficial for the future, but is also quite advantageous while we are in the body. After all, perfect health is vulnerable and liable to reversal if the body grows fatigued and cannot support the weight of health. Beware of spitting out water now and later desiring a drop, like the rich man.[55] No one experiences a hangover from drinking water. No one's head hurts if it is saturated with water. No one needs another's feet if he spends his life drinking water. No one trips over his own feet, no one loses the use of his hands, if he imbibes water. For digestive problems, which are the necessary consequence of self-indulgence, produce terrible maladies in the body.

[54]See Lk 16.19–31.
[55]See Lk 16.24. Garnier comments on this line: "I would like you to note that the use of both meat and wine was prohibited in Lent, and because of this here only water is mentioned."

The one who fasts has a venerable complexion, not florid with shameless blushing but adorned with a modest paleness. His eyes are gentle, his gait calm, his countenance thoughtful. He does not mock with unbridled laughter. His speech is measured and his heart pure. Remember the saints of old, *of whom the world was not worthy,*[56] who *went about in skins of sheep and goats, destitute, afflicted, ill-treated.*[57] Remember them in order to imitate their way of life, if indeed you seek their portion. What gave Lazarus rest in the bosom of Abraham?[58] Wasn't it fasting? The life of John was a single continuous fast: he had neither a bed, nor a table, nor arable land, nor a steer for ploughing,[59] nor grain, nor a miller, nor anything else that pertained to livelihood.[60] Hence *among those born of women there has risen no one greater than John the Baptist.*[61] The fasting that Paul names when boasting over his afflictions brought him up to the third heaven.[62]

But our Lord is the principal example among those already mentioned. Only after he fasted to fortify the flesh that he assumed for our sake did he receive in it the devil's assaults.[63] In this, he not only instructed us to fast in order to prepare[64] and train ourselves for struggles with temptation, but also gave his adversary a kind of

[56]Heb 11.38.
[57]Heb 11.37.
[58]See Lk 16.23.
[59]Garnier noted (PG 31.177 n. 45) that Erasmus had inserted *ut ait Hesiodus* after these words, but has harsh words for him: "Basil is not calling that poet to mind, but the man of great and nearly infinite reading wanted to indicate that Basil, when he said 'a steer for ploughing,' had borrowed this phrase from Hesiod." Ducaeus (PG 31,1795b) identified the reference as *Works and Days* 405–410: "First of all, get a house, and a woman and an ox for the plough—a slave woman and not a wife, to follow the oxen as well—and make everything ready at home, so that you may not have to ask of another, and he refuse you, and so, because you are in lack, the season pass by and your work come to nothing" (Trans. Hugh G. Evelyn-White). It seems that if in fact there is any allusion to Hesiod here, it is rather a kind of "counter-allusion."
[60]See Mt 3.4.
[61]Mt 11.11.
[62]See 2 Cor 11.27; 12.2.
[63]See Mt 4.2.
[64]See n. 32 above on ἀλείθει.

foothold by his abstinence. For the sublimity of our Lord's divinity would have prevented the devil from gaining access to him if he had not descended to the human condition through abstinence. Nonetheless, he availed himself of food before ascending to the heavens in order to confirm the nature of the resurrection body.[65]

But what about you? Aren't you letting yourself grow enormously fat and obese?[66] Are you placing no value on the salvific and life-giving doctrines when you cause your mind to waste away from want of such nourishment?[67] Or do you not know that, just as in battle joining forces with one side achieves the defeat of the other, so too the one who has joined the side of the flesh prevails over the spirit and the one who has switched to the side of the spirit enslaves the flesh? *For these are opposed to each other.*[68] Hence if you wish to make your mind strong, subdue your flesh through fasting. Indeed, this is what the Apostle says: the more *the outer man wastes away*, the more *the inner man is renewed*.[69] And: *When I am weak, then I am strong.*[70]

Why won't you despise the food that doesn't last forever? Why won't you foster the desire for the table in the kingdom, for which fasting here and now prepares you in every way? Do you not know that by excessive self-indulgence you produce a fat worm that tortures you? Indeed, whoever received a share of any spiritual gift in the midst of abundant food and continuous self-indulgence? In order to receive the law a second time Moses needed to fast a second time. The Ninevites would not have escaped the destruction with which they were threatened if the irrational animals had not fasted along with them.[71] *Whose bodies fell in the wilderness?*[72] Was it not

---

[65]See Lk 23.43.
[66]Cf. Basil, *Second Homily on Fasting* 8.
[67]Ibid.
[68]Gal 5.17.
[69]2 Cor 4.16.
[70]2 Cor 12.10.
[71]See Jon 3.4–10.
[72]Heb 3.17; cf. Num 14.29, 32–33.

those who desired to eat meat? As long as they were content with manna and water from the rock, they conquered the Egyptians, and they travelled through the sea. *In their tribes were none who fell behind.*[73] But when they remembered the fleshpots and returned to Egypt in their hearts,[74] they did not see the promised land. Doesn't this example make you afraid? Doesn't gluttony make you shudder, for fear of being excluded from the goods for which we hope? Then again, the wise Daniel would not have seen visions if he had not made his soul lucent through fasting. For the vapors emitted by coarse food, being as it were sooty and black, disrupt the illumination of the mind produced by the Holy Spirit like a dense cloud.

Furthermore, if the angels have any food, it is bread, as the Prophet says: *Man ate the bread of angels*[75]—neither meat nor wine nor anything else eagerly sought by the slaves of the stomach. Fasting is a weapon used in the fight against the demons. *For this kind is not expelled save by prayer and fasting.*[76] While the goods of fasting are so great, self-indulgence is the beginning of arrogance.[77] For self-indulgence and drunkenness and every variety of rich food is swiftly accompanied by every kind of bestial licentiousness. Thus

[73]Ps 105.37 (104.37 LXX).

[74]See Ex 16.3.

[75]Ps 78.25 (77.25 LXX).

[76]Mk 9.29.

[77]Gk. ὁ δὲ κόρος ὕβρεων ἀρχή. See Basil, *Second Homily on Fasting* 6. Ducaeus (PG 31.1795c) detects here an allusion to a saying of Solon preserved by Diogenes Laertius 1.59: "Self-indulgence is born of riches, but arrogance is born of self-indulgence." Ducaeus is correct in identifying this line as a proverb, but probably not correct in identifying its source. Diogenes Laertius has mangled the saying attributed to Solon (Fr. 6; preserved by Aristotle, *Constitution of Athens* 12.2): "For self-indulgence begets arrogance when much wealth comes near men whose mind is not suitable." A very similar saying attributed to Solon's contemporary Theognis of Megara: "For self-indulgence begets arrogance when wealth comes near the bad man whose mind is not suitable." The proverb that self-indulgence begets insolence is mentioned by Aristotle in *Protrepticus* fr. 4; Philo, *On Abraham* 228; *Special Laws* 3.43; *On the Virtues* 162. Finally, Clement of Alexandria quoted the lines of both Solon and Theognis, though in abbreviated form, omitting from "men" or "man" onward (*Stromata* 6.2.8.7–8). Hence Basil could have encountered this proverb in any of these authors, or elsewhere.

men became *horses in heat*[78] because of the sting of lust which self-indulgence produces in the soul. Inversions of nature arise when people are drunk; they seek the male in the female and the female in the male. Fasting also recognizes limits for marital relations; by checking excess in what is customarily conceded, fasting fosters agreed-upon leisure so that they may persevere in prayer.[79]

10 Nonetheless, do not define the good derived from fasting only in terms of abstaining from food. For true fasting is being a stranger to vice.[80] *Loose every bond of wickedness.*[81] Let your neighbor grieve you; forgive him his debts.[82] Do not *fast only to quarrel and fight.*[83] You do not devour meat, but you devour your brother. You abstain from wine, but you have not mastered your arrogance. You wait until evening to partake of food, but you spend your day judging others. Woe to those *who are drunk, but not with wine!*[84] Anger is a drunken state of the soul because, like wine, it robs the soul of sense. Sadness, too, is a drunken state because it drowns the mind. Fear is another drunken state, when things happen that should not happen. For it says: *deliver my soul from fear of the enemy.*[85] Generally speaking, since each of the passions disturbs the mind, each can rightly be called a drunken state of the mind.

Think of the person who rages with anger, how he is drunk with the passions. He lacks self-composure. He lacks awareness of both himself and those around him. As if in some nocturnal battle, he lunges at everyone and trips over everything. He talks wildly and cannot be restrained. He rails, he assaults, he menaces, he swears, he shouts, he erupts. Flee this drunkenness! But neither should you give yourself over to the drunkenness that comes from wine. Do not

[78]Jer 5.8.
[79]See 1 Cor 7.5.
[80]Cf. Basil, *Second Homily on Fasting* 7.
[81]Is 58.6.
[82]Cf. Mt 6.12.
[83]Is 58.4.
[84]Is 51.21.
[85]Ps 64.2 (63.2 LXX).

anticipate drinking water by drinking wine.[86] Do not let drunkenness initiate you into the fast. Drunkenness is not the doorway to fasting. After all, the doorway to righteousness is not rapaciousness, the doorway to moderation is not licentiousness, and to sum up, the doorway to virtue is not vice. There is no other way to enter into fasting. Drunkenness leads to licentiousness, sobriety to fasting. The athlete prepares by training, the one who fasts by practicing self-control.

Do not acquire a hangover immediately before these five days, as if you were avenging these days or outsmarting the legislator. Indeed, you toil in vain if you wreck your body but do not comfort it with abstinence. Your storehouse is treacherous.[87] *You draw water in a leaky jar.*[88] After all, the wine will pass through you and exit along its own path, but the sin remains. A household slave runs away from the master that beats him. But you remain with the wine that beats your head each day. The use of wine is best measured by the body's need. But if you exceed this boundary, you will arrive tomorrow afflicted with a headache, yawning, dizzy, reeking of vomited wine.[89] It will seem to you as if everything is whirling around, as if everything is wobbling. While drunkenness induces a slumber akin to death, it produces a wakefulness like dreams.

11 Do you know, then, whom you will welcome as your guest? He who promised us: *I and the Father will come and make our home with him.*[90] So then, why are you anticipating his arrival with drunkenness and closing the door to the Master? Why are you urging your

[86]Gk. μὴ προλάβῃς πολυποσίᾳ τὴν ὑδροποσίαν. Garnier notes that two mss read οἰνοποσίᾳ in place of πολυποσίᾳ, which he thinks to be "best and especially fitting," but prefers πολυποσίᾳ based on other mss. In any case, they mean more or less the same thing.

[87]That is, the stomach. Cf. Basil, *Second Homily on Fasting* 7.

[88]A common proverb for laboring in vain derived from the punishment assigned to the Danaids in Hades; see Xenophon, *Oeconomicus* 7.40; Plato, *Gorgias* 493b; Aristotle, *Politics* 1320a32. Basil cites it elsewhere: *Mund* 3 and *Litt* 9.

[89]Cf. Basil, *Second Homily on Fasting* 4.

[90]Jn 14.23.

enemy to occupy your fortifications before his attack? Drunkenness does not provide a welcome for the Lord. Drunkenness drives away the Holy Spirit. After all, as smoke drives away bees, so a hangover drives away spiritual gifts. Fasting brings about the orderliness of a city, the tranquility of the forum, the peace of households, the security of possessions. Do you want to see its nobility? Compare this evening with tomorrow evening, and you will see that the city has exchanged tumult and storminess for a deep calm. Indeed, I pray that today be like tomorrow in terms of nobility but that today's frivolity not carry over to tomorrow.

The Lord has brought us to this period of time. May he grant that we, like competitors, display the steadiness and vigor of perseverance in these preliminary contests and so arrive at the appointed day of coronation. Let us now recollect the saving passion but in the age to come may we be rewarded for our actions throughout life by the righteous judgment of Christ himself, to whom be glory forever. Amen.

Second Homily on Fasting

1 *Comfort the people, you priests! Speak to the ears of Jerusalem!*[1] Speech is of such a nature that it has the ability to increase the desires of the eager and to awaken the eagerness of the lazy and sluggish. Thus after generals have arranged their army into a battle line, they give an encouraging speech before the battle begins, and their exhortations have such power that quite often they produce contempt of even death in the majority. And as trainers and coaches escort their athletes to contests in stadiums, they exhort them vehemently about the necessity of toiling for the crowns, such that many of them are convinced to disdain their bodies out of ambition for victory. And indeed, though it falls on me to array the soldiers of Christ for the war against invisible enemies and to prepare the athletes of piety for the crowns of righteousness through self-control, even I need a word of encouragement.

So then, brothers, what I am saying? That it is valid for those who practice on a regular basis and train hard in wrestling academies to fatten themselves with plenty of food, so that they can engage in their toils with greater vigor? Rather, I am saying that those to whom it is said: *the fight is not against blood and flesh, but against principalities, against powers, against the rulers of the world of this darkness, against the spirits of wickedness,*[2] need to be trained for the contest through self-control and fasting. While oil fattens the athlete, fasting strengthens the practitioner of piety.[3] Hence the more you deny the flesh, the

---

[1]Is 40.1–2. Basil has altered the scriptural text considerably: *Comfort, comfort my people, says God. You priests, speak to the heart of Jerusalem.*

[2]Eph 6.12.

[3]Gk. τὸν ἀσκητὴν τῆς εὐσεβείας. This could also be translated "the ascetic of piety."

73

more you render the soul radiant with spiritual health. For it is not the body's tone but rather the soul's perseverance and steadfastness in affliction that results in strength against invisible enemies.

2 So then, fasting is beneficial at all times for those who undertake it. For the demons dare not hurl abuses at the one who fasts, and the angels who diligently guard our life stand beside those who purify their soul through fasting. And even more so now, when the summons to fast has been announced to the whole world. There is no island, no mainland, no city, no people, no remote place which does not hear the summons. Rather soldiers, and travelers, and sailors, and merchants all likewise hear the announcement and receive it with great joy. No one should remove himself from the register of those who fast, in which all peoples and all ages and all ranks of dignity are counted. It is angels who register them in each church. If you take a little pleasure in food, beware of losing your place in the angels' register and having the one who raises the army consider you liable to an indictment of desertion. It is less dangerous to be convicted of abandoning your weapons in battle than to be seen abandoning the great weapon of fasting.

Are you rich? Do not mock fasting, deeming it unworthy to welcome as your table companion. Do not expel it from your house as a dishonorable thing eclipsed by pleasure. Never denounce yourself to the one who has legislated fasting and thereby merit condemnation to bitter penury caused either by bodily sickness or by some other gloomy condition. Let not the pauper think of fasting as a joke, seeing that for a long time now he has had it as the companion of his home and table. But as for women, just as breathing is proper and natural for them, so too is fasting. And children, like flourishing plants, are irrigated with the water of fasting. As for seniors, their long familiarity with fasting makes a difficult task easy. For those in training know that difficult tasks done for a long time out of habit become quite painless. As for travelers, fasting is an expedient companion. For just as self-indulgence necessarily weighs them down because they carry around what they have gorged themselves with, so too fasting renders them swift and unencumbered. Furthermore, when an army is summoned abroad, the provisions the soldiers take are for necessities, not for self-indulgence. Seeing that we are marching out for war against invisible enemies, pursuing victory over them so as to hasten to the homeland above, will it not be much more appropriate for us to be content with necessities as if we were among those living the regimented life of a military camp?

3 Endure suffering like a good soldier, and contend like a professional athlete, so that you may be crowned,[4] all the while knowing this, that everyone who contends exercises self-control in all things.

But just now as I was saying this, something occurred to me that does not deserve to go unmentioned. The provisions of worldly soldiers are increased in proportion to their exertions, whereas the spiritual warrior who has less provisions has more honor. And so, our *helmet*[5] differs in nature from their corruptible one: theirs is made of copper, whereas ours is made of *the hope of salvation*.[6] Their shield is made of wood and hide, but our defense is *the shield of faith*.[7] We are protected by a *breastplate of righteousness*,[8] but they wear chainmail. And we have the *sword of the Spirit*[9] for our defense, but they wield a sword of iron. Thus it is clear that we are not strengthened by the same provisions as they are: the doctrines of piety strengthen us, whereas they need their stomachs filled.

So then, since the temporal cycle has brought us to these days, which we miss as dearly as our nurses from long ago, let us all welcome them with gladness. The church uses these days to nurture us in piety. Therefore, you who are about to fast should not look gloomy like the Jews, but beautify yourself in accordance with the gospel, not

[4]Cf. 1 Cor 9.25.
[5]1 Thess 5.8.
[6]Ibid.
[7]Eph 6.16.
[8]Eph 6.14.
[9]Eph 6.17.

despondent over the emptiness of your stomach but rather delighting in your soul because of the spiritual joys.[10] For you know that *the desires of the flesh are against the spirit and the desires of the spirit are against the flesh.*[11] So then, since they are opposed to one another, let us diminish the comfort of our flesh and boost the strength of our souls, so that through fasting from the passions we may achieve victory and be rewarded with the crowns of self-control.

4 So then, right now you need to make yourself worthy of the seriousness of fasting, lest you ruin tomorrow's self-control by today's drunkenness. "Since it's been announced that five days of fasting are coming upon us, today let's drown ourselves in drink."[12] What an evil thought! What a wicked idea! No one about to enter into a legitimate marriage with a woman first shacks up with concubines and whores. Nor does a legitimate wife tolerate shacking up with such degenerates. So likewise, when fasting is on the horizon, your first response should not be to get drunk. For drunkenness is the universal harlot, the mother of shamelessness, the lover of the absurd, the frenzied woman who is prone to every form of disgracefulness.

Indeed, fasting and prayer have no place in the soul defiled by drunkenness. The Lord welcomes inside the sacred precincts the one who fasts but refuses admission to someone nursing a hangover as impure and unclean. After all, if you were to arrive tomorrow reeking of wine and vomit, how could I consider your hangover as fasting? Don't offer the excuse: "I've not filled my cup with undiluted wine recently!" Realize that your system is still not cleansed of wine. Where should I put you? With the drunks? Or with those who fast? A past inebriation still holds one in its grip; a present hunger testifies to fasting. Your drunkenness makes you the subject of dispute, like an enslaved prisoner of war. Providing clear evidence of your enslavement, it will not keep you—and rightly so—from smelling like wine, as if it were still in its jug.

[10]Cf. Mt 6.16–18.

[11]Gal 5.17.

[12]Here Basil refers to a five-day fast. See above, *First Homily on Fasting,* n. 52.

The first day of your fast will immediately meet with disapproval because of the lingering effects of your drunkenness. That the beginning of your fast meets with disapproval and the whole of it is rejected is clear: *Drunkards will not inherit the kingdom of God.*[13] If you were to come to fasting drunk, what benefit is it for you? Indeed, if drunkenness excludes you from the kingdom, how can fasting still be useful for you? Don't you realize that experts in horse training, when the day of the race is near, use hunger to prime their racehorses? In contrast you intentionally stuff yourself through self-indulgence, to such an extent that in your gluttony you eclipse even irrational animals. A heavy stomach is unconducive not only to running but also to sleeping. Oppressed by an abundance of food, it refuses to keep still and is obliged to toss and turn endlessly.

5 Fasting protects children, chastens the young, makes seniors venerable. For grey hair is more venerable when it is adorned with fasting. It is an adornment very well suited for women: it restrains those in their prime, guards the married, nourishes virgins. Such is how fasting is practiced privately in homes. But how it is practiced in our public life? It disposes every city as a whole and all its people to good order, quiets shouting, banishes fighting, silences abuse. What teacher's arrival settles down the uproar of boys as abruptly as the advent of fasting quells the tumult of the city? What reveler carries on when fasting? What band of lascivious dancers is formed by fasting? Silly giggling and obscene ditties and erotic dancing abruptly leave the city, banished by fasting as if by a stern judge.

Now if all were to take fasting as the counselor for their actions, nothing would prevent a profound peace from spreading throughout the entire world. Nations would not rise up against one another, nor would armies clash in battle. If fasting prevailed, weapons would not be wrought, courts of justice would not be erected, people would not live in prisons, nor would there ever be any criminals in the deserts, any slanderers in the cities, or any pirates on the sea. If

[13]1 Cor 6.10.

all were students of fasting, they would never hear *the voice of the taskmaster*[14] mentioned in the book of Job. Nor would our life be so lamentable and sorrowful if fasting were to preside over our life. For it is clear that it would have taught all people not only to control themselves with regard to food, but also to completely avoid and be utterly estranged from avarice, greed, and every kind of vice. When these are extirpated, nothing can prevent us from passing our life in profound peace and tranquility of soul.

6 Now those who reject fasting and pursue self-indulgence as if it were the source of life's happiness have opened the way to that great swarm of vices and destroy their own bodies as well. Please observe the difference in the faces of those whom you will see tonight and those whom you will see tomorrow. Tonight their faces will be swollen, flushed, and dripping with beads of sweat; their eyes watery, droopy, and deprived of sharp perception due to an internal cloudiness. But tomorrow their faces will be serene and stately, restored to their natural color and full of intelligence; their eyes sharp in every perception since no internal cause obscures their natural operation.

Fasting is likeness to the angels, companionship with the righteous, moderation in life. It made Moses the lawgiver. Samuel is the fruit of fasting. Hannah as she fasted vowed to God: *O Lord God of Sabaoth, if you were to look upon your maidservant and give me a male child, then I will offer him in your presence as a gift. He shall drink no wine or strong drink until the day of his death.*[15] The great Samson was reared on fasting, and as long as it was part of that man's life, his enemies fell by the thousands,[16] the gates of the city were pulled down,[17] and lions did not withstand the strength of his hands.[18] But when drunkenness and fornication seized him, he was easily captured by his enemies. And after he was deprived of his eyes,

[14]Job 3.18.
[15]1 Sam 1.11 LXX.
[16]Judg 15.16.
[17]Judg 16.3.
[18]Judg 14.6.

he was set out as a plaything for little Philistine boys. After Elijah fasted, he shut up heaven for three years and six months.[19] For when he saw that such great arrogance had been born of self-indulgence, he deemed it necessary to subject them to involuntary fasting with a famine, forcing an end to their sin, which had already increased beyond measure. It was fasting that, like a kind of cauterization or amputation, halted the rampant spread of vice.

7   Take fasting, O you paupers, as the companion of your home and table; O you servants, as rest from the continual labors of your servitude; O you rich, as the remedy that heals the damage caused by your indulgence and in turn makes what you usually despise more delightful; O you infirm, as the mother of health; O you healthy, as the guardian of your health. Ask the physicians, and they will tell you that the most perilous state of all is perfect health. Accordingly experts prescribe going without food to eliminate excessive eating lest the burden of corpulence destroy the body's strength. For by prescribing not eating food to eliminate intemperance, they foster a kind of receptivity, re-education, and fresh start for the redevelopment of the nutritive faculty. Hence one finds the benefit of fasting in every pursuit and in every bodily state, and it is equally suitable for everything: homes, fora, nights, days, cities, deserts. Therefore, since in so many situations fasting graces us with something that is good in itself, let us undertake it cheerfully, as the Lord said, not looking gloomy like the hypocrites but exhibiting cheerfulness of soul without pretense.[20]

And yet I do not think that I need as great an effort to encourage someone to fast as I do to discourage someone today not to fall into the evil of drunkenness. For indeed while many undertake fasting because of custom and peer pressure, I dread drunkenness because drunkards cling to it as a kind of paternal inheritance. Just like those who sail away for a long journey, today some of these idiots buy wine for the

[19]1 Kg 17.1.
[20]Cf. Mt 6.16–18.

five days of fasting.[21] Who is so idiotic that, even before he starts to drink, he is already out of his mind like a drunk? Doesn't he know that the stomach does not keep down what is deposited in it? It is treacherous to enter into a contract with the stomach! Being a storehouse that contains many things and yet unguarded, the stomach retains the injury done to it, but does not keep down what is deposited in it.

Avoid having what was just read said to you, if you should arrive drunk tomorrow: *I have not chosen this fasting, says the Lord.*[22] Why do you mix what cannot be mixed? What partnership has fasting with drunkenness? What communion has intoxication with self-control? *What agreement has the temple of God with idols?*[23] For if the temple of God is where the Spirit of God dwells,[24] then those who permit the filth of licentiousness to enter into themselves through drunkenness are the temple of idols.

Today is the vestibule of fasting. Doubtless he who has been defiled in the vestibule is not worthy to enter into the sanctuary. No household servant who wants to regain the favor of his master employs his enemy as his patron and mediator. Drunkenness is inimical to God, but fasting is the beginning of repentance. So then, if you wish to return to God through repentance, flee drunkenness lest it render your alienation from him all the more bitter. Nonetheless, abstinence from food by itself is insufficient for praiseworthy fasting. Rather, we must fast with an acceptable fasting that is pleasing to God. True fasting is being a stranger to vice, controlling the tongue, abstaining from anger, distancing oneself from lust, evil speech, lying, perjury. The absence of these vices makes fasting true, and so shunning these vices makes fasting good.

8   Let us *take delight in the Lord*[25] by meditating on the utterances of the Spirit and by undertaking the precepts of salvation and all

[21]See note 12 above.
[22]Is 58.5.
[23]2 Cor 6.16.
[24]Cf. 1 Cor 3.16.
[25]Ps 37.4 (36.4 LXX).

the teachings aimed at the emendation of our souls. Yet let us be on guard against the interior fast.[26] The Prophet prays for it to be averted, saying: *The Lord will not let the souls of the righteous go hungry.*[27] And: *I have not seen the righteous man forsaken or his children begging for bread.*[28] Since he knows that the children of our patriarch Jacob descended into Egypt for bread, he is not speaking about perceptible bread, but rather he is speaking about the spiritual food by which our interior man is perfected. May the fast with which the Jews were threatened not come upon us: *Behold, the days are coming, says the Lord, and I will send a famine upon this land, not a famine of bread, nor a thirst for water, but a famine of hearing the word of the Lord.*[29] It was for this reason that the Just Judge sent it, because he saw their mind wasting away from a lack of the nourishment that comes from the doctrines of truth, yet their external man was growing enormously fat and obese.

And so, in all the coming days the Holy Spirit will give you a feast at both the morning and evening festivities. No one should willingly absent themselves from this spiritual banquet. Let all of us share in the sober cup. It has been prepared by Wisdom, who hands it to us equally, to the extent that each has the capacity to drink it. *For she has prepared her cup and slaughtered her beasts,*[30] that is, *the food for the perfect, for those who have their faculties trained by practice to distinguish good from evil.*[31] Filled with such an abundance, may we be found worthy too of the joy experienced in the bridegroom's chamber, in Christ Jesus our Lord, to whom be glory and might forever and ever. Amen.

[26]Gk. ἀπο μέντοι τῆς ἐν τῷ κρυπτῷ νηστείας φυλαξώμεθα.
[27]Prov 10.3.
[28]Ps 37.25 (36.25 LXX).
[29]Am 8.11.
[30]Prov 9.2.
[31]Heb 5.14.

Homily Against Drunkards

1   The spectacles of this evening move me to speak, but then again
the futility of previous efforts check my impulse and blunt my
willingness. For even a farmer, when his first batch of seeds has not
germinated, is quite reluctant to spread a second batch in the same
fields. In the past we encouraged you continuously and then night
and day during these seven weeks of fasting we testified to you cease-
lessly about the gospel of the grace of God: If so many exhortations
have proved to be of no benefit at all, then what should we expect if
we preach today? O how many nights have you kept vigil in vain?
How many days have you assembled in vain? Indeed, in vain! He
who has made progress in good works, then relapses into old habits,
not only suffers the loss of the reward for his labors, but also merits
heavier condemnation. Even though he tasted the good word of God
and merited knowledge of the mysteries, he forsook everything,
baited by fleeting pleasure. *For the least of all men may be pardoned in
mercy, but mighty men will be mightily tested.*[1] A single evening and
a single assault of the enemy destroyed and obliterated all that labor!
So then, am I willing to speak now? I would have kept silent, trust
me, if I had not feared the example of Jeremiah. When he did not
want to address the disobedient people, he suffered the very things
he himself described: a fire came into his heart, he was weakened in
every way, and he could not bear it.[2]

Lewd women, who forget the fear of God and scorn the everlast-
ing fire, on that day when they were supposed to be sitting in their
homes in remembrance of the resurrection, reflecting on that day

[1]Wis 6.6.
[2]See Jer 20.9.

when the heavens will be opened and the Judge will appear to us out of the heavens, as well as the trumpets of God, and the resurrection of the dead, and the just judgment, and the repayment to each according to his deeds—lewd women, instead of pondering these things in their mind, purifying their hearts of wicked thoughts, washing away their past sins with tears, and preparing themselves to meet Christ on that great day of his appearing,[3] instead of doing these things they shook off their yoke of slavery to Christ, ripped the veils of modesty from their heads, despised God, despised his angels, acted shamelessly at the sight of every male, tousling their hair, *dragging their garments in trains and at the same time tinkling with their feet*,[4] incited frenzied dancing with their lascivious eyes and boisterous laughter, enticing young men to commit every form of licentiousness with them, formed bands of dancers in the martyr's shrines in front of the city and made the holy places a workshop for their own obscenity. They defiled the air with their obscene ditties,[5] defiled the earth with their unclean feet, stomping on it while dancing, and drew a crowd of young men into a circle of spectators around themselves: they were truly insolent and totally carried away, omitting no excess of insanity. How could I keep silent about such things? How could I bemoan them as much as they deserve? Wine has caused us the loss of these souls; though wine is the gift God gave to the sober as a comfort for infirmity, it has now become an instrument of licentiousness for the lascivious.

2 Drunkenness is the demon of our own choosing, entering souls through pleasure. Drunkenness is the mother of wickedness, the antithesis of virtue. It turns the brave man into a coward, the chaste man into a lecher. Righteousness it knows not; prudence it destroys. For as water counters fire, so too does an excessive amount of wine extinguish rationality. And so, I was reluctant to say something

[3]See Acts 2.20; Jude 1.6; Rev 6.17, 16.14.
[4]Is 3.16 LXX.
[5]Cf. Basil, *Second Homily on Fasting* 5.

against drunkenness, not because it is an insignificant vice or worth overlooking, but because whatever I say would produce no benefit at all. For if the drunkard is out of his mind and in a stupor, whoever rebukes him goes through this rigmarole in vain since he does not hear a thing! So then, to whom shall we preach? For the one who needs exhortation does not hear what is said, but the one who is chaste and sober does not need the assistance provided by what I say, since he is free from passion. So then, what shall I do in these circumstances, when speaking is useless and silence problematic? Should we neglect to care for them? But negligence is dangerous. Then again, shall I say something against drunkards? But our words ring in dead ears. So then, perhaps, just as in times of pestilence those who care for bodies fortify the healthy with preventive remedies, but do not touch those who have succumbed to the disease, so too what I say can be useful for half of you: it can provide a safeguard for those not under the influence, but cannot provide relief and healing for those who have succumbed to the disease.

3 How do you differ, O man, from irrational brutes? Isn't it by the gift of reason, which you received from the one who created you, that you became the ruler and lord of all creation? So whoever has deprived himself of his wits through drunkenness *is compared to senseless beasts and becomes like them.*[6] In fact, I would say that those in a drunken state are even more irrational than beasts. For all quadrupeds and beasts have the impulse to mate at appointed times, but those whose soul is seized by drunkenness and whose body is filled with unnatural heat are driven at every opportunity and at every hour to impure and disgraceful intercourse, and to pleasures. And not only does this produce brutish irrationality in them, but also the perversion of their senses shows that the drunkard is worse than every beast. For what beast's vision and hearing is as distorted as a drunkard's? Don't they fail to recognize their closest kin and frequently run up to strangers as if they were intimate friends?

[6]Ps 49.12 (48.13 LXX).

Don't they frequently jump over shadows as if they were streams or gullies? Their ears are filled with sounds like the roaring of the billowing sea. The ground seems to rise uphill and the mountains appear to circle around them. Sometimes they cannot stop laughing, sometimes they are pained and wail inconsolably. Now they are courageous and undaunted, now terrified and cowardly. They find sleep onerous, insufferable, suffocating, and in fact bordering on death, but when awake they are in more of a stupor than when asleep. For their life unfolds in a dream: they have neither coat nor anything to eat the next day, yet in their drunkenness they rule like a king and lead armies, build cities, and distribute goods. It is the wine seething in their hearts that fills them with such fantasies and such great delusion. But others come round to the opposite passions: they lose all hope, and become downcast, distressed, teary, frightened at every noise, and easily scared. The same wine in different bodily situations effects different passions in souls. For in some it can cause a diffusion of blood which flushes the surface of the body, rendering them cheerful and pleasant and glad. But in others it causes an oppressive condition which contracts and compresses their blood, bringing them round to the opposite disposition. And what need is there to speak of the throng of the other passions? Discontentment? Irritability? Querulousness? Volatility? Shouting? Uproar? Gullibility? Rage?

4   A lack of self-control with respect to pleasures is quick to arise from wine, like water suddenly welling up from a spring—and undiluted wine is swiftly accompanied by the malady of lasciviousness.[7] This malady demonstrates that every madness which beasts have for females takes second place to the lust of drunkards. For irrational brutes recognize the boundaries of their nature, but drunkards seek the female in the male and the male in the female. Nor is it easy to enumerate verbally all the awful things that happen because of

[7]Here Basil plays on *akrasia*, "lack of self-control," and *akratos*, "undiluted wine."

drunkenness. So then, while the harmful effects of plague are experienced by people over time since the air infects bodies with its own corruption little by little, the harmful effects of wine are experienced immediately. For after drunkards have so destroyed their soul that they are branded with every kind of stigma and blemish, even still they also destroy the very condition of the body. Not only do they languish and waste away because of excessive indulgence in those pleasures that make one crazy for sex, but also because of the burden that this places on them they lug around a body that is flaccid and flabby and robbed of its vital tone. Their eyes are reddened. They are sallow in appearance. They breathe with difficulty. Their tongue is loose. Their shouting is unintelligible. Their feet stumble like those of children. They have accidental excretions of waste products, which trickle as if from irrational brutes.

Because of their self-indulgence they are pitiable. They are more pitiable than those storm-tossed on the sea, who wave after wave submerges and keeps from rising above the surf. The souls of drunkards are similarly swept underwater when submerged in wine. And so, just as storm-tossed ships, whenever they become full of water, must lighten themselves by jettisoning their cargo, so too must drunkards unload themselves of whatever weighs them down. But they are hardly freed from what loads them down by vomiting and spitting up! Drunkards are more pitiable than those sailing on dangerous waters insofar as the latter blame winds, the sea, and external forces, but the former willingly choose to enter the storm of drunkenness. Whoever is possessed by a demon is pitiable, but whoever is drunk, even though he suffers the same things, does not deserve our pity because he wrestles with a demon of his own choosing.

Furthermore, those in a drunken state[8] concoct drugs, not out of a scheme to avoid the terrible suffering that comes from wine, but rather to prolong their drunkenness indefinitely. For they find the day short, and the night and the winter brief, at least insofar as time for drinking is concerned. But their wickedness has no end.

[8]Here I follow the alternative reading μέθῃ instead of μέθης.

For wine leads to more wine. It does not satisfy a need, but produces an inexorable need for another drink, making those who are drunk thirsty and arousing in them an ever-greater appetite for more. But even though they imagine that they have an insatiable desire for drink, they experience or rather deliberately choose something quite the opposite of this. For by continual self-indulgence they dull their senses. Just as too much light blinds the eyes, and those buffeted by loud noises are made completely deaf by the excessive beating that their ears suffer, so too drunkards fail to notice that they destroy whatever pleasure they experience by their excessive love of pleasure.[9] They find the wine tasteless and watery even if it is undiluted. And when in its place they drink fresh wine, they find it warm, even if it is completely unmixed, even if it is ice-cold, and it cannot quench that internal fire that burns within them from an excessive amount of wine.

Who has woe? Who has confusion? Who has quarrels? Who has bouts of nausea and gossip? Who has afflictions without cause? Who has redness of eyes? Is it not those who pass their time in wine, those who scope out where the drinks are?[10] Now *woe* is an interjection that expresses lament. And so, those who are drunk deserve lament because *drunkards will not inherit the kingdom of God.*[11] They have *confusion* because of the mental disturbance that wine produces. And they have *bouts of nausea* because of the bitterness that the pleasure of drinking distributes throughout their bodies. For the use of their feet is hampered, even the use of their hands is hampered, because drunkenness delivers fluid to these members. And yet even before they suffer these things, at the very moment they drink they are suffering inflammations of the brain.[12] For when the cerebral membranes become saturated with the fumes emitted by exhaled wine, the head is stricken with unendurable pains. Unable to remain upright upon the shoulders, the head flops around on the vertebrae,

[9]See Basil, *Second Homily on Fasting* 8.
[10]Prov 23.29–30.
[11]1 Cor 6.10.
[12]Lit. *phrenitis.*

now dropping here, now sinking there. *Gossip* refers to the excessive talking and contentious debates found at drinking parties. Finally, *afflictions without cause* happen to the intoxicated, seeing that they are unable to stand up straight on account of their drunkenness. For they slip and fall down in so many different ways that their bodies cannot avoid suffering *afflictions without cause.*

5   But who could say such things to drunkards? They have headaches from their hangover, they're half-asleep, they yawn, their eyes are foggy, and they're nauseous. In such a state they pay no regard to their teachers, who shout at them from all directions: *Do not get drunk on wine, in which lies dissipation!*[13] And again: *Wine leads to licentiousness, and drunkenness to arrogance!*[14] Disregarding these teachings, they willingly experience the effects of drunkenness. Their body becomes swollen, their eyes moist, their mouth dry and parched. For just as ravines appear full while running with torrents of melted snow, but are left dry once all the water has passed by, so too the body[15] of an intoxicated person is, as it were, full and moist when a pool of wine is formed in it, but is exposed as dry and devoid of moisture once even a little of the wine has flowed away. But when the body is continually overwhelmed and inundated by an excessive amount of wine, it also loses its vital humor. For what human constitution is so strong that it can withstand the evils of drunkenness? How could a body continually heated and continually sodden by wine avoid becoming exhausted and enfeebled and depleted? Hence the trembling and weakness: for when their breath grows short because of an excessive amount of wine and the tension of their sinews relaxes, the whole mass of their body is overcome by tremors. Why do you call the curse of Cain upon yourself, seeing that you tremble and wander in a stagger all through life?[16] For the body that lacks physical steadiness cannot avoid quivering and tottering.

[13]Eph 5.18.
[14]Prov 20.1.
[15]Reading τὸ σῶμα (Maran) instead of τὸ στόμα (Garnier).
[16]See Gen 4.11–14.

6 How long wine? How long drunkenness? You risk being mud instead of a human being since you are so completely mixed with wine and rot along with it, reeking of wine from your daily hangover—and vomited wine at that—as if you were an utterly useless vessel. Isaiah mourns for these people: *Woe to those who rise early in the morning and pursue strong drink, who tarry therein until the evening: wine shall consume them! They drink their wine to the accompaniment of harp and flutes, but they do not consider the works of the Lord nor ponder the works of his hands.*[17] Among the Hebrews it is customary to call every drink that can cause drunkenness "strong drink." So then, there are some who search around for places where drinks are found as soon as the day breaks, make the rounds of the wine shops and taverns, invite each other to go drinking, and expend all their mental energy in pursuit of such things: it is these people whom the Prophet bemoans. For they leave themselves no opportunity for pondering the wonders of God. Their eyes have no leisure for looking up to the heavens and observing the beautiful objects therein, for studying every orderly arrangement in beings, so that from the good order of these things they may form a notion of the Creator. Rather, as soon as the day breaks they immediately adorn the places for their *symposiums*, or drinking parties, with multicolored carpets and floral wall hangings, and display eagerness and diligence in the preparation of the vessels, arranging the *psykters*, the *kraters*, and the *phiales*,[18] as if assembling them for a kind of procession or sacred festival. Thus they conceal their indulgence through a variety of vessels and sufficiently prolong their time for drinking by the alteration and exchange of vessels.

[17] Is 5.11–12. The list of accompanying instruments is abbreviated: "to the accompaniment of harp, and psaltery, and drums, and flute . . ." This may be a transcriptional omission.

[18] Here Basil lists the vessels traditionally used at a Greek *symposium*, or drinking party. The *krater* was a large jar in which the wine was mixed with water to dilute it before being drunk. The *psykter* was a mushroom-shaped vessel that was filled with wine and placed in a *krater* full of cold water or ice in order to cool it before mixing it. The *phiale* was a round, shallow, saucer-like bowl used to pour libations.

At these drinking parties there are *symposiarchs* who preside, as well as head cup-bearers and table-waiters: they bring about a semblance of order in disorder and of organization in chaos. And so, just as the presence of bodyguards boosts the dignity of civic leaders, so too the attendants stationed around the wine as if it were a kind of empress conceal its ignominy with the greatest possible zeal. In addition, garlands, and flowers, and perfumes, and incense, and innumerable other trifles create even more preoccupation for those who are perishing. Then as the drinking proceeds, quarrels, arguments, and disputes break out over who gets more to drink since they aspire to surpass each other in drunkenness. But the devil presides at these games, and sin is the reward for victory. For whoever pours out more undiluted wine carries away the victory prize from the others. Truly, *they glory in their shame*.[19] For while they vie with each other, they inflict harm on themselves. What could I say that would get through to those who have become so shameless? Everything brims with irrationality, everything brims with confusion. The defeated get drunk, the victorious get drunk, the attendants mock them. The hand falls limp from exhaustion, the mouth can take no more, the stomach bursts, but the evil does not diminish. The wretched body, having lost its natural tone, is dissipated in every way, unable to withstand the violence brought on by excess.

7   What a pitiful spectacle for Christian eyes! A man who is in the prime of life, vigorous in body, pre-eminent in the military ranks, is carried home on a stretcher, able neither to stand up nor to walk on his own feet! A man who ought to make his enemies tremble with fear sparks the laughter of boys in the forum! He has been stricken, but not by a sword; he has been slain, but not by enemies. A man-at-arms at the very pinnacle of his life has become a casualty of wine, ready to suffer according to the whim of his enemies. Drunkenness is the eradication of rational thoughts, the obliteration of strength, decrepitude before its time, imminent death. After all, what are

[19]Phil 3.19.

drunkards other than the idols of the nations? *They have eyes, but they do not see; they have ears, but they do not hear.*[20] Their hands are paralyzed; their feet are numb. Who has plotted such things? Who is the cause of these evils? Who has concocted this drug of madness for you? O man, you have turned your drinking party into a battlefront. You remove the young men from battle, leading them by the hand as though they were wounded, in that you brought death to the flower of youth with wine. And you invite him to a meal as a friend, but you send him away dead, in that you have snuffed out his life with wine.

Whenever they believe themselves to be saturated with wine, it is then that they begin to drink, and they drink in the manner of cattle, that is, as if from a spring close at hand that sends up as many streams as the number of those reclining at table. For even before the drinking began, a certain young man joined them. He was noble in bearing, not yet drunk, and carried a large *phiale* of chilled wine. He knocked their cup-bearer out of his way, stood in the middle of the room, and by means of curved straws doled out drunkenness to his fellow *symposiasts* in equal measure. This novelty is the standard of excess, insofar as they join each other in debauchery to an equal degree, with no one surpassing the other in drinking. For once the tubes have been distributed and each takes the one before him, they drink without breathing, like cows as if from a kind of cistern: the harder they suck the wine into their throats, the quicker the *psykter* discharges it to them from above through the silver pipes.

Look down at your wretched stomach. Notice the size of the cup that you have received, that its capacity is nearly a half-pint.[21] Do not look at the wine-decanter[22] in the hope of draining it soon; rather, look at your own belly; see that it already full. And so, *woe to those who rise early in the morning and pursue strong drink, who*

[20]Ps 115.5–6 (113.13–14 LXX).

[21]Lit. *cotyla*, a Greek liquid measure that ranged from 8.5 to 9.5 fl. oz., or about a half-pint.

[22]Lit. *oenochoe*, a pitcher used to take wine from the *krater* and pour it into the cups.

tarry therein until the evening[23] and pass their day in drunkenness.[24] For they give themselves no opportunity to *consider the works of the Lord nor ponder the works of his hands.*[25] *Wine shall consume them!*[26] For when the heat caused by wine is present in the body, it becomes the spark that ignites the arrows of the enemy. While wine douses reason and intellect, it arouses passions and pleasures as if a kind of swarm of bees. For what chariot drawn by foals is not[27] driven in a disorderly manner when its driver has been thrown off? What ship that is without a steersman and tossed by waves as if by chance is not safer than a drunkard?

8   Because of such evils, men and women jointly form mixed bands of dancers,[28] hand their souls over to the demon of wine, and thereby wound each other with the arrows of passion. The giggling on the part of both sexes, their appalling ditties, and their obscene gestures inflame lewdness. Tell me, do you giggle and delight in licentious delights, even though you should be weeping and groaning over your past actions? Do you sing obscene ditties, discarding the psalms and hymns that you were taught?[29] Do you move your feet, and leap around like a madman, and dance with those who ought not dance, even though you should be bending your knees in adoration? For whom should I lament? For the unmarried maidens? Or for those constrained by the yoke of marriage? After all, the former have returned without their virginity, but the latter have not returned their conjugal chastity to their husbands. Even if one way or another some of them avoided sinning with their body, nonetheless they welcomed corruption into their souls with open arms.

[23]Is 5.11.
[24]Cf. Prov 23.30.
[25]Is 5.12.
[26]Is 5.11.
[27]Here I emend οὕτως to οὐκ.
[28]See Basil, *Second Homily on Fasting* 5.
[29]It seems better to translate this sentence as interrogative, not indicative.

Let me apply what I have said to the men. Has one of them leered? Has one of them ogled?[30] *Whoever looks upon a woman in order to lust has already committed adultery.*[31] If accidentally encountering women is so dangerous for those whose eyes wander around carelessly, how much more dangerous is it to meet with women deliberately to watch them behaving disgracefully from drunkenness, making erotic gestures, and singing dissolute songs? Merely hearing these songs can produce every kind of frenzy for pleasure in licentious people! What will they say? How will they defend themselves? From such spectacles they round up a swarm of innumerable evils. Haven't they have looked for this reason, that they might rouse lust? So then, according to the inescapable verdict of the Lord, they are liable to the condemnation of adultery.

How will Pentecost welcome you, when Pascha has been treated with such disrespect? Pentecost made the coming of the Holy Spirit evident and known to all. But in anticipation of it you made yourself a habitation of the adversary spirit and became a temple of idols, instead of becoming a temple of God through the indwelling of the Holy Spirit. You have provoked the curse of the Prophet, who spoke in the person of God: *I will turn their feasts into mourning.*[32] How will you rule your household servants when you yourselves are enslaved to foolish and harmful desires as if you were prisoners of war? How will you reprove your children when you live a life that is deaf to reproof and devoid of regulation? What then? Shall I abandon you in this situation? But I fear that whoever lacks discipline somehow may become even more perverse,[33] that whoever is pricked with compunction *may be overwhelmed by excessive sorrow.*[34] For it says: *healing will make great sins cease.*[35] Let fasting cure your drunkenness.

---

[30]It seems better to translate these two sentences as interrogative, not indicative.

[31]Mt 5.28.

[32]Am 8.10.

[33]Gk. στραγότερος, "more perverse." Some mss read ῥᾳθυμότερος, "more careless."

[34]2 Cor 2.7.

[35]Eccl 10.4.

Let psalms cure your obscene songs. Let tears heal your giggling. Instead of dancing, bend the knee. Instead of clapping your hands, strike your breast. Instead of the adornment of clothing, humility. In all things let almsgiving redeem you from sin.[36] For *the ransom of a man is his own riches.*[37] Form into a community of prayer the many who are afflicted, in the hope of being forgiven for the wickedness you have dreamt up.

When *the people sat to eat and drink, and rose up to play*[38] (now the playing here is idolatry),[39] then the Levites took up arms against their brothers[40] and consecrated their own hands to the priesthood.[41] So then, as for you who fear the Lord, however much the disgraceful conduct of the condemned has now caused you distress, this is the command we give to you: If you see that they repent of the foolishness of their past actions, have compassion for them as you would for your own bodily members when they are sick. But if they are obstinate and scorn your sorrow for them, *go out from among them, and separate yourself from them, and do not touch what is unclean.*[42] In this way, those who feel shame may come to recognize their own wickedness, but you may receive the reward of the zeal of Phineas, through the righteous judgment of our God and Savior Jesus Christ, to whom be glory and might forever and ever. Amen.

[36]See Dan 4.27 LXX.
[37]Prov 13.8.
[38]Ex 32.6.
[39]See Ex 32.7–24.
[40]See Ex 32.26–28.
[41]See Ex 32.29.
[42]2 Cor 6.17.

On Giving Thanks

1 You have heard the Apostle's saying, which he taught to the Thessalonians as a rule for all of life. Indeed, the teaching is for everyone, whatever their condition in life; the profit extends to all humankind. *Rejoice always*, he says; *pray without ceasing; give thanks in all circumstances.*[1] What joy consists of, what profit comes from it, how one can apply the duty to pray without a gap and thank God for everything, this we will now describe in detail. And we must also refute the objection of the adversary, who here blasphemes by insisting that this teaching is impossible to perform.

"What good is it," such a doubter asks, "to spend the time, night and day, cheerful and merry in spiritual mind games? How can these be possible when we are surrounded by a multitude of unanticipated troubles that give the soul inevitable grief, whereby it is all the more impossible to rejoice and be cheerful? Should we be like one who is being roasted on a gridiron and perceives no pain, or goaded and feels no torment?"

Perhaps someone here today, in the sickness of his mind, is seeking a pretext for sin, and dares, because of his laziness in observing the commandment of the lawgiver, to cast blame by suggesting that these things are impossible. "How is it possible," he is thinking, "for me to rejoice always, especially as joy is caused by external circumstances and does not rest with us? After all, joy results from the arrival of friends, extended time with parents, discovery of some treasure, public honor, recovery from a severe illness, and anything else that makes for a happy life: a well-supplied house, an abundant table,

---

[1] 1 Thess 5.16–18. Scriptural citations follow the translation of the New Revised Standard Version unless noted otherwise (cf. *On Baptism*, note 1).

merry and companionable friends, agreeable sounds and spectacles, health of close relatives, and other signs of life's success. And that which distresses us is not just what happens in our own life, but also what befalls friends and relations. These also contribute to whether the soul is happy and cheerful. We also want to see our enemy fail, the downfall of the persecutor, fair dealings with our benefactor, and that no unexpected mishaps provoke or alarm our life; then the soul can rest joyful. Why are we given a command to observe that does not depend on the will, but on these other circumstances? How can I, moreover, pray without ceasing, with all of life's needs and wants making a necessary claim on the soul's attention, when it is impossible for the soul to address two concerns at the same time?

2   "And further, to give praise in all things is going a bit too far for me," he continues. "Should I give thanks when someone tortures me? Whips me stretched out on a wheel? Rips out my eyes? Should I give thanks when my persecutor dishonors me with ill treatment? When I am dying of cold, consumed with hunger, bound to the rack, deprived of children or spouse? Should I give thanks when shipwreck suddenly strips me of goods? When I am beset by pirates on the sea, or highway robbers on the road? Give thanks, when I am damaged by false accusations? Wandering? Housed in prison?"

By complaints such as these—and many others—the lawgiver's accuser seeks to justify his sins, even going so far as slander, claiming that the teaching we are given is impossible to accomplish.

How do we respond? I say that such an argument is quite contrary to the vision of the Apostle, whose intention is to raise up our soul—which is now creeping about in a sinful fog, rolling on the earth and in the flesh like a worm in the mud and failing to appreciate the lawgiver's exalted mind—to a heavenly way of life. He not only invites those who are enjoying what is good to rejoice always, but also those who no longer live in the flesh, in whom Christ lives, who for the highest good permit no association with the burdens of the flesh. Indeed, should their flesh suffer, the afflictions of the body cannot have any effect on the soul, if we kill these earthly members by the Apostle's teaching, and bear the death of Jesus Christ in our life; the wounds that would kill the body do not spread to the soul, its association having been severed. Thus it is that insult, punishment, death of relatives cannot trample the spirit nor upend the lofty soul into suffering. Those in this frame of mind, who are pulled into some distress, will have little sorrow as they endure painful misfortune. But those who live according to the flesh are to be pitied, not for their misfortune, but because they did not choose to do what they ought. A perfect soul, once it has been touched by the desire for its Creator, will rejoice here and now in a beauty, joy, and delight not shaken by the twists and turns of sinful desire. In fact, what causes others grief will only strengthen the joy of such a person.

This was the mind of the Apostle, who rejoiced in weakness, distress, beatings, violence, boasting in what made him weak:[2] in *hunger and thirst, in cold and nakedness*,[3] in persecution and anguish, what was unbearable to others, and made them weary of life. Indeed, the ones who do not know and share the Apostle's conviction, with his admonition to the gospel life, dare to complain against Paul, saying that this command is impossible for us. They must learn how many opportunities God's generosity offers us to a reasonable joy.

He has called us into existence out of nothing, created in his image, our nature made perfect, giving us the sense and reason by which we perceive God. Let us attentively consider the beauty of creation, reading in it, in large letters, the great Providence of God and his wisdom over all things. We are capable of distinguishing good from evil and can learn from nature to choose what is useful and to turn away from what will do us harm. Alienated from God by sin, we are liberated from shameful servitude through the blood of the Only Begotten. From this we have the hope of the resurrection, participation in the goodness of the angels, and a comprehension that is beyond anything we might be able to put into words.

[2] 2 Cor 12.10.
[3] 2 Cor 11.27.

3   How can anyone deny that these are cause for perpetual joy and contentment, but suppose instead that the pleasure-filled life belongs to the one who serves the belly, delights in music, and rolls around and snores in bed? I would go so far as to say that reasonable people should pity the sort of person who lives for the present. Blessed, rather, are those who exchange the present for the hope of the life to come. When with God, whether we are sitting in flames like the three young men in Babylon,[4] locked up with lions,[5] or swallowed by a sea monster,[6] we must nonetheless give praise, rejoicing and not mourning over the present, but be merry in the hope of what is to come. Equipped for holy combat, I must endure the assaults of the enemy in expectation of glory, looking forward to the immortal crown.

The one who has undergone gymnastic training will not be disheartened in the arena when he gets hit, but will immediately attack the opponent, despising momentary affliction in order to be named the champion. So also, when those who love virtue encounter something unpleasant, it will not hinder their joy. For *suffering produces endurance, and endurance produces character, and character produces hope, and hope does not disappoint us.*[7] Therefore the Apostle exhorts us, in another place, to rejoice in hope and hope in distress.[8] It is hope that produces a soul rejoicing in virtue. The same Apostle exhorts us to *weep with those who weep,*[9] and in the letter to the Galatians he mourned *the enemies of the cross of Christ.*[10] And need we mention that Jeremiah wept, and that Ezekiel mourned for those who suffered God's punishment: *Woe is me, my mother, that you bore me;*[11] *Woe is me, for the faithful have disappeared from the land and there is no one left who is upright;*[12] and *Woe is me, for I have*

[4]Dan 3.19–23ff.
[5]Dan 6.16ff.
[6]Jon 1.17.
[7]Rom 5.3–5.
[8]Rom 12.12.
[9]Rom.12.5.
[10]Although Basil cites Galatians, his quote in fact follows Phil. 3.18.
[11]Jer 15.10.
[12]Mic 7.2.

become like one who gathers straw at the harvest.[13] Examine closely all of these sayings of the righteous, and you will be convinced that they all scorn this world and life's misery. *Woe is me that my pilgrimage endures so long*.[14] [Paul] demands to be released from this life and be with Christ.[15] He laments the extension of this journey in life as a hindrance to joy. David, in his Psalm, laments over the death of his friend Jonathan, at the same time also lamenting his enemy: *I am distressed for you, my brother Jonathan*;[16] and *Daughters of Israel, weep over Saul!*[17] He mourns by name him who was killed in sin, and Jonathan, while he was his lifelong best friend. What need do we have for further examples? The Lord wept over Lazarus[18] and over Jerusalem.[19] And he blesses those who mourn[20] and also those who weep.

4 But, you ask, how do we reconcile this with the command to rejoice always? Tears and joy do not come from the same source. Tears arise[21] from some unexpected event that strikes the soul and stuns it, constricting the breath around the heart. In joy, the soul leaps, exulting in some thought. Both imprint themselves differently on the body. Sorrow creates a pallor, appearing pale as lead and cold; joy, on the other hand, creates a blooming, rosy appearance, as if the soul cannot be contained but is pressing to burst out. From this we can say that the complaints and tears of the holy ones arise out of love for God. They see, always, the Beloved, and this increases their joy. In sympathy with their fellow servants, they experience sorrow when they sin and correct them through their tears. Those who stand on

[13]Mic 7.1.
[14]Ps 120.5 (119.5 LXX).
[15]Phil 1.23.
[16]2 Sam 1.26.
[17]2 Sam 1.24.
[18]Jn 11.35.
[19]Lk 19.41.
[20]Mt 5.4.
[21]Here Basil explains the human need to weep in terms of his understanding of the medical physiology of tears. See also the last section in chapter five, below.

the shore have sympathy for those who are shipwrecked, but without putting their own safety in danger by their concern. It is the same way with one who grieves over the sins of his neighbors but without losing his own joy. In fact, tears over the brother reap the joy of the Lord: *Blessed are those who weep*; and *Blessed are those who lament*, for *they will be comforted* and *they will laugh*.[22] It is called laughter but it is not that which bursts forth out of red and engorged cheeks. Rather, it is pure cheerfulness unhampered by sorrow. The Apostle permits us to weep with those who weep because one such tear is like a seed and pledge of eternal joy. Lift up your mind with me, and consider the life of the angels, whether it is not composed of genuine joy and delight, seeing that they stand before God and enjoy the inexpressible beauty and magnificence of our Creator. It is to this life that the Apostle encourages us, while ordering us to rejoice always.

5   But as for the Lord weeping over Lazarus and the city, we say this: He also ate and drank, not because he needed to, but in proportion and limit, that you might renounce the natural sensations of the soul. He also wept, that those who are disposed to immoderate sorrow might regulate their lamentation and tears. For if our tears are to be in reasonable moderation, it is necessary to assess the circumstances: who, how, when, and in what manner they are fitting. Thus the Lord wept without excessive passion as an example for us, adding these words, *Our friend, Lazarus, has fallen asleep, but I am going there to awaken him*.[23] Who among us bewails a sleeping friend, one he believes will shortly awaken? *Lazarus, come out!*[24] And the dead man came to life, and the bound one walked forth. Wonder of wonders! The feet were bound with cloth wraps and yet unhindered from coming forward. The power was greater than the constriction. How now should the Lord, able to do such things, have valued lamentation of this event? Or is it not obvious that he always com-

[22]Lk 6.21; Mt 5.5.
[23]Jn 11.11.
[24]Jn 11.43.

mands proportion and purpose to the natural sensations, to help accommodate our weakness? He did not express emotion like some wild animal; he disdains immoderate lamentation and weeping as something base. Therefore in his grief over his friend, he proves his participation in human nature, not permitting that we should surrender ourselves to the grosser weakness of affection, nor that we let some sorrowful occurrence make us senseless. In the same way, the Lord was able also to perceive hunger and thirst, his muscles and sinews experiencing weariness with the exertions of his travels, without him being in any way moved in his divinity, since it was the body that was susceptible to influence according to its nature. In the same way, he also produced tears, permitting to the flesh that which corresponded to its nature.

For tears are caused when sorrow fills the cavities in the head with vapor, and the accumulated moisture is propelled out through the canals of the eyes. If we hear unexpected distressing news, it causes a ringing in the head, dizziness, dimmed vision, the head trembling from the vapors that are being pressed out as a result of the accumulated internal heat. That which has been blocked up is released, the thick vapors distilled into tears, as rain comes from clouds. This is how the person who weeps out of grief experiences a sort of pleasure in tears, as the internal pressure is relieved. Daily experience confirms this. We know from the example of many who are struck with terrible misfortune but who hold back the force of their tears, that many afterwards suffer incurable illness, paralyzed even to death by the blows they experienced. Deprived of relief, their strength was broken as a consequence of their sorrow. It is like fire that suffocates when the smoke is not allowed to draw; this also happens when the life force, unable to exhale, is extinguished as a result of grief.

6   This is why those who are prone to sorrow must not use the Lord's tears as an excuse for their passions. The fact that the Lord enjoyed food is no excuse for our gourmet tastes, but rather defines for us the outermost boundaries allowed for abstinence and frugality. So, too, his tears don't mean that we must weep, but rather provide us with a suitable measure and prescribe a specific principle: that we remain within the proper bounds of nature in the manner in which we suffer distress. Neither women nor men are permitted to weep beyond what is due. One may grieve over misfortune and weep to a certain degree, in a tempered way, without loud complaints and screams, without tearing the clothing or strewing oneself with ashes, or doing any other unseemly things not in accord with what is taught about the things of heaven. For the one who is refined through godly teaching must act from right reason, as if guarded by a wall that wards off the passions through courage and constancy, and not like someone in a ditch who permits the sorrowful and effeminate soul to let loose a swarm of passions. Such a weak soul indeed derives no strength from hope in God, but permits itself to be crushed down and overcome with misfortune. As worms are produced in soft wood, so also melancholy is fostered by the soft human feelings.

Did Job have a heart as hard as a diamond? Were his guts[25] made of stone? He lost ten of his children in a brief moment, who were annihilated at one blow while enjoying themselves in a beautiful house, when Satan caused the place to fall down in ruins. He saw the table sprinkled with blood. He saw the children, of different ages but sharing in a common fate. And yet he did not lament, tear out his hair, or curse. Instead, he spoke those renowned and universally acclaimed words of thanksgiving: *The Lord gave and the Lord has taken away; blessed be the name of the Lord.*[26] Was he a man without any sympathy? Can this be? For it says about Job that he *wept over all those in affliction.*[27] Was he lying? Not at all. It testifies truly about him, him who was true above all other virtues. *The man*, it says, *was blameless, righteous, godly, and true.*[28]

[25]Gk. σπλάγχνα.
[26]Job 1.21.
[27]Job 30.25.
[28]Job 1.1.

But you, on the other hand, serve yourselves with mournful songs, full of lamentations, and you seek to soften your soul through such dirges. In addition to this, just as an actor alters his posture and dress while on stage, so you think you must show your grief with a particular appearance: black clothing, torn hair, a dark house, dirt, dust, and keening, perpetually picking at the wounds of sorrow in the soul. The one given over to such display has no hope. But you are above such theatricals, since you are taught about the one who has fallen asleep in Christ that *What is sown is perishable, what is raised is imperishable. It is sown in weakness, it is raised in strength; it is sown a physical body, it is raised a spiritual body.*[29] Why are you lamenting over someone who has simply changed his clothes? You need not lament as if you have lost all help for your life. As it is written, *It is better to hope in the Lord than to hope in man.*[30] You need not bemoan the dead like one struck with some terrible blow. The celestial trumpet will soon wake him up, and you will see him appear before the throne of Christ. Away, too, with every vulgar and coarse exclamation: "O what unexpected disaster! Who would have believed that this could happen? How could I have thought that someone I loved so dearly would end up buried in the dirt?" We ought to blush if we hear such things; we need only to remember the past as well as present experience to know that we cannot escape misfortune.

7   For these reasons we should never be crushed by either untimely death or by the occurrence of some unexpected unpleasantness, if we are truly God-fearing. "I had a son," you say. "He was my only heir, my security for my old age, the pride of the family, the best of his peers, the support of his house, he stood in the bloom of his age. This one death has taken from me. He, who such a short time ago spoke so beautifully, was the delight of his father's eye, has now become earth and dust! What should I do? Should I tear my clothing,

[29]1 Cor 15.42–44.
[30]Ps 118.9 (117.9 LXX).

roll about in the dirt, and complain and lament and in the presence of others have a tantrum like some child who, receiving punishment, screams and kicks? Or should I consider the inevitability of such an event: that the law of death is unavoidable; that it strikes those of every age, gradually claiming all; that to be overcome in this way is nothing out of the ordinary and not as one who lets his courage fail when hit with an unanticipated blow? Indeed I had known long in advance that I, being mortal myself, had a mortal son, that nothing human will continue, and no property is held forever."

Great cities, renowned for their architecture and the might of their peoples, cities that excelled in wealth, land, and trade, now lie in ruins, everything once fine about them now buried in loss. Often, too, a ship, after weathering a thousand storms, its captain entrusted with countless wares, is utterly wrecked by a single typhoon. Also, a military force, one known for its victories, when fortune shifts, is ruined in rumor and spectacular defeat. Indeed, whole nations and islands that have gained power over water and land, having amassed immense wealth, in the course of time either fall into ruin or are conquered, losing their freedom.

In short, no evil can take place that has not already happened in the past. We compare weights by placing them in a balance, and discern the quality of gold by testing it with stone. In the same way, when we think about all that the Lord has ordained, we should not let ourselves respond beyond the boundaries of moderation. If you encounter something unpleasant, your spirit has been prepared, so that you need not be shaken up, the hope of things to come making light your present misfortune. Just as one with weak eyes turns them away from anything that is very bright, refreshing the vision with flowers and herbs, so also must your soul not stare at sorrow, fixating on present afflictions, but rather focus your eye on the true Good. If you do this, you will come to that place where you rejoice always, that is to say, where your conduct is always right with God and the hope of reward lightens life's distresses.

Has someone insulted your honor? Well then, turn your focus to the glory that is bequeathed in heaven for patience. Have you suffered a loss of your assets? Well then, look to the wealth and treasure you have gathered in heaven through your good works. Are you deprived of your native land?[31] Well then, the heavenly Jerusalem is indeed your native land. Have you lost a child? Well then, you have the angels, with whom you may gather around the throne of God and rejoice eternally. If you set present suffering against future good, you will prove your soul firm in the face of sorrow and disturbance, as the command of the Apostle admonishes. Do not yield to immoderate joy when you have worldly success, nor let sorrow, through dejection and alarm, suppress your joy and good spirits. If you do, you have not been properly instructed as to life's proportions; you will never have a calm and storm-free life. You can bear it lightly when you have this teaching as your companion, the teaching that instructs you to perpetual joy. Cast off, therefore, the burdens of the flesh and take on the joy of the soul; in so doing, you will elevate yourself above earthly things and direct your spirit to the hope of eternal good, satiating the soul with joy, and maintaining angelic bliss in our hearts in Jesus Christ our Lord, to whom be glory and might unto eternity. Amen.

[31]Gk. πατρίς.

On the Martyr Julitta

(AND ON GIVING THANKS, CONCLUDED)

1 The reason for this assembly[1] is to commemorate the blessed martyr, manly in a woman's body, who amazed both those who witnessed the event as well as everyone who hears her story in later times. The most blessed woman, Julitta—if, indeed, one might call her a woman, such a great soul concealed within the weakness of her female nature—was, through our common foe, struck with that which is most insufferable for women to overcome. His praise and arrogance would overturn entire cities, upending the world like one who seizes a nest and heaves out the abandoned egg; but he found himself vanquished by a woman's virtue. During the trial at which he attempted to undermine her weak nature, she preserved her piety to the end. Indeed, the trial proved her to be the stronger of the two, and the more he thought to intimidate her with torture, the more she laughed at his terrorism.

The facts are these: She had a lawsuit with a powerful man in the city. He was a greedy, violent creature who had amassed his wealth through theft and plunder. This man seized much of her property, good fields and farms, cattle and slaves, and all that she owned. Then he bribed witnesses to lie and convinced a corruptible judge to take the court case. On the appointed day, when the witnesses and defense were gathered, the woman began to expose the injustices, prove their sort and their method, the enduring legitimacy of her claim on the property, and her entitlement to justice, lamenting the man's violence and greed.

[1]Gk. ἐκκλησία.

But then he stepped forward and said that she had no right to bring the case to court. "Those who do not worship the gods of the emperor," he said, "have no recourse to lawsuits unless they are willing to renounce their faith in Christ." The judge considered this statement fair and just, and immediately ordered incense and a bowl for sacrifice, instructing the plaintiff that she need only renounce Christ and she would enjoy legal protection. But, he warned her, if she persisted in such beliefs, she would have no civil rights, either in the court or in the law.

2   What did she do? Did she want to regain her wealth? Did she abandon her dispute? Was she frightened by the danger, threatened by the judge? By no means. Rather, she said, "Away with life; away with possessions! I would rather lose my life than speak a single word against God my maker!"

Her words inflamed the judge's anger to a pitch of frenzied wrath, as she repeatedly thanked God, turning the dispute over temporal goods to a focus on heavenly property and the privilege of exchanging earth for paradise, considering that the present shame would win her a crown of glory. Being deprived of temporal life, she would gain the blessed hope, receiving health along with sanctity in the joy of the heavenly kingdom. And so, as she was interrogated, she repeatedly identified herself as a servant of Christ and cursed those who demanded that she deny her faith. The unjust judge announced that he would deprive her not only of the goods that had been stolen from her, but her life. In other words, he meant that she was to be burned alive.

But Julitta hurried forward quickly to the fire, as if running to some sweet pleasure. Her countenance and her posture proved the truth of her words, with a visible serenity in her high spiritual rapture. She exhorted the women who were standing nearby to be willing to suffer misery for the sake of the faith, not to tremble like weak women, and not to yield to the frailty of their nature. "We are made of the same stuff as men," she said. "We are made in the likeness of God just as they are. The woman is made by the Creator to be just as capable of virtue as men. How is this so? Are we not related in every way? For not only was the woman made by taking flesh from the man, but also bone from his bone. Do we not then have the same obligation to the Lord as men, to be as constant in courage and patience?"

After she had said these things, she leapt onto the funeral pyre. The body of that holy one was then encircled, as if in some splendid bridal chamber. Her soul was sent over into the heavenly fatherland and its deserving rest. Her venerable body, on the other hand, was preserved for her relatives, undamaged. This body was interred in the most beautiful narthex of the city's church, sanctifying both the place and those who come to flock around it. The earth itself was blessed by receiving the blessed one, sending up a pure fountain of water for souls. Thus the martyr became like a mother, nursing those in the city on her communal milk. This spring serves as a prophylactic for those who are healthy, a source of pleasure for those who are self-controlled, and comfort for the sick. The martyr provides us with the same benefit that Elisha once gave to the inhabitants of Jericho, where he transformed the region's naturally salty water, by his blessing making it sweet and wholesome.

I say to you men: Do not fall short of the example of this woman in your piety! And women: Do not prove yourselves weaker than her example, but hold fast to your piety without excuses, through hearing her story. Do not permit a soft nature to hinder anyone from doing good.

3   I would say more about the martyr, but the sermon that I began yesterday remains unfinished, and so does not permit me to dwell on her any longer, especially since I have a natural aversion to leaving anything unfinished. A half-finished painting is not very appealing, and the discomforts of travel are pointless if the traveler does not reach the intended goal and appointed lodgings. In the same way, a hunt that yields nothing more than some paltry piece of game is hardly better than nothing, as is losing a race, especially if the prize is lost because one falls short by a single step.

And so I would like now to tease out a little more detail than we considered yesterday, on why the teaching is so necessary, and fill a few gaps with things that still need to be said.

The Apostle said, we remember, *Be joyful always, pray without ceasing, give thanks in all circumstance.*[2] What I said yesterday about always rejoicing is enough for a summary, but more is necessary to treat the subject with suitable dignity. Whether we must also pray without ceasing, and whether we can actually fulfill this command—these are the things that you want to hear now from me, and my task is to explain them as fully as possible.

Prayer is a demand that the faithful makes to God to obtain some particular good. Such desires are not limited to words. After all, we do not believe that God needs to be reminded by words; he knows what is good for us without being asked. So what should we say? Limit prayer not to syllables, but to the intentions of the soul, and a lifelong practice of virtue. This is the fullness of prayer's power. *Whether you eat,* he says, *or drink, or whatever you do, do everything for the glory of God.*[3]

When you sit down for a meal, pray. As you take bread, thank the Giver. When you are strengthening your weakened body by drinking wine, thank him who bestowed on you such a gift to cheer your heart and fortify your infirmities. As you get dressed, thank him for what he has given you. When you wrap your cloak around your shoulders, so increase your love for God, who has provided us with clothing suitable for winter and summer, to maintain our life and cover us modestly. Is the day at an end? So thank him who gave us the sun by which we can perform our daily work, and fire to enlighten the night, and who has bestowed on us all the rest of life's needs. The night gives us other opportunities for prayer. Look up to the heavens

---

[2] 1 Thess 5.16–18. Scriptural citations follow the translation of the New Revised Standard Version unless noted otherwise (cf. *On Baptism*, note 1).

[3] 1 Cor 10.31.

and consider the beauty of the stars, and so give prayer to the Lord of visible things, and worship the Creator of all, who has made all by his wisdom. When you see living creatures dropping off to sleep, so again worship him, who cuts short our labors by forcing us into sleep, thus providing us with new strength through a brief rest.

4   But we should certainly not devote the entire night to sleep. Don't lose half of your life in sluggish slumber. Instead, divide the hours of the night between sleep and prayer. Sleep, in fact, ought to be a continuation of your devotional practices. For the images that we see in our sleep are largely echoes that follow our waking worries; thus our activities when we are awake will necessarily correspond to our dreams. So then, you will pray without ceasing when you offer prayer that is not restricted to words, but also uniting it with God in all that you do in life. Indeed, your life should become an unceasing and uninterrupted prayer.

But the Apostle also says, *Give thanks in all circumstances*. And how, one asks, is this possible? How can a soul, crushed low by disasters and pierced with grief, avoid bursting out with complaints and tears over things that are truly terrible? Should one give thanks as if receiving a blessing? When something happens in my life that my enemy wants for me, how can I give thanks for it? If a mother has a child snatched away prematurely, so that she is wounded by sorrow more bitter than labor pains, her heart grieving over the loved one, how should she suspend her complaints for words of thanks? How?

By saying this: The child she bore has God as its true father, and God is a wise protector and counselor. Why not let ourselves yield entirely to the action of such a wise master rather than complaining when we are robbed as if it is our property, and pitying the dead as if they have suffered some great injustice? Consider, instead, that the child is not dead but rather given back; that the friend does not face death but is merely on a journey, following a route that we too must take, but going his way a little ahead of us. Let God's command be your companion for the road, a steady flame and light to discern the heart. Proceed with this principle as a guide for your soul, a guard over every thought, so that you cannot be shaken by what happens in life; instead, your mind will be like a rock in the sea, one that endures the wind and waves without moving.

Why are you not more joyfully accustomed to the fact that mortals come from mortals? Why is the death of your child such a surprise? If someone had asked you when your son was first born what the child was, how would you have answered? Would you have said it was anything other than a human being? But if it is a human being, then it is obviously going to die. What is so offensive when a mortal dies? Don't you see the sun rise and set? Don't you see the moon wax and wane? Doesn't the earth turn green and then become dry? What in the world around us lasts forever? What remains unchangeable and unshaken in its essence? Watch the heavens and observe the earth; not one of these things remains eternal. *The heavens and the earth will pass away*, said the Lord. *The stars will fall from heaven; the sun will be darkened; the moon will not give its light.*[4] So what is the marvel if part of this universal fate descends on you? Agree to endure it with patience, not as if you feel nothing[5] or have no sensations at all[6]—these would be symptoms of stupidity—but with effort and under a thousand sorrows. Stand firm, as a brave athlete does, not only to prove his strength and courage while he dispatches his opponent, but also to resist firmly the strikes he receives. The most intrepid ship's pilot is all the wiser for his long experience; he never permits his courage to drop, and stands firm as he defies every storm. The bereavement of a beloved child, a dear wife, or a beloved friend and kind relative has nothing that can fearfully disturb the person who is intelligent and able to rightly judge how to govern his own life. It is beasts that are distressed by separation from what is familiar. I have seen an ox weep when his yoke-partner died. One can

[4]Mt 24.29.
[5]Gk. ἀπαθῶς.
[6]Gk. ἀναιθήτως.

see that even dumb beasts form shared affiliations. There is nothing improper about cultivating a friendship as a result of conversations and long daily association. But when you go your separate ways, it is hardly reasonable if you start wailing just because you have known each other for a long time.

5   Say, for example, a wife is taken from you by sudden death. She has been your life companion, sweetened your existence in every possible way, through her cheer, her ability to radiate joy in the household, and her economical thrift. Do not be angry about the adversity. Do not condemn what happened as fate, as if there is nothing governing this world. Do not think that the creator must be evil, nor adopt any such pernicious doctrine that abandons true faith. Yes, you were two in one flesh, and it is inevitably painful to experience such a division and dissolution of this bond. But you gain no profit by thinking or speaking in this way. Consider, instead, that God who has shaped us and given us breath has also conferred on each individual a particular lifespan: according to one person this, to another that hour of death. So for one it is arranged that the soul will remain in the body a little longer, while another is more quickly liberated in accordance with God's unutterable wisdom and righteous word. We might compare it with those thrown into prison. One languishes for a long time in the torment of his shackles, but another is released more quickly. In the same way, some souls have a longer stay in this life while others live more briefly, each person granted whatever is most suitable according to the foresight of our creator in the depths of his wisdom, something no human mind can grasp. Did you not hear David say, *Deliver my soul out of its prison*?[7] Have you not heard from the Holy One that your soul would be unfettered?[8] What did Simeon do when he took the Lord up in his arms? What words did he speak? Did he not say, *Now let your servant be dismissed, O Lord*?[9]

[7] Ps 142.7 (141.8 LXX).
[8] Tob 3.6.
[9] Lk 2.29.

For the one who is hastening to heaven, the sojourn in the body is more difficult than a beating and imprisonment. So do not order your soul according to whatever you please. Keep in mind that the effect of death on life's associations is a separation that might be compared with travelers who are going along the same road together in perpetual conversation and shared habits, and then part from one another. When you are on a common road and you come to a cross-roads where you must go separate ways, you do not just stand there, mindless of your intended goal. Instead, you remember why you are traveling, why you started out on your journey, and then were thrown together in your common direction. Although the shared journeys had different purposes, a friendship developed along the way. So, too, is the one affiliated with another through marriage or any other of life's associations. Each has its predetermined time, and when one arrives at the end, it is time to part.

6   This is how the person will behave who has insight about such partings. He will not take leave unwillingly, but rather will thank the one who first made the companionship possible. But you, when you had them, did not thank the giver for such gifts—your friend, your child, whatever it is you lost and now lament. If you lived with a wife, you complained that you had no children. If you had children, you complained that you were not wealthy, or that others enjoyed wealth. Beware lest a love for fine living makes it something we "need," so that we fail to value the present until it is too late. If we do not thank God for the good that he gives us in the present, we will be forced to appreciate its value when he takes it away from us. Just as the eye may sometimes fail to focus on what is too close, and needs a moderate distance, so too is the ungrateful soul deprived of past good in order to become conscious of its benefit. For when they had the good, they did not in any way admit the grace of what had been given, but only understood its blessing when it was taken away.

Yet no one is without some reason to give thanks, if he has any sense. Life gives each of us many different experiences, and we might take the opportunity to contemplate deeper values and the worth of the good we possess by comparing it with those whose measured allotment is worse than our own. Are you a slave? Certainly there must be someone lower than you; thank God that you have a degree of superiority, that you are not, say, condemned to the games, or that you are not beaten. But the slave in those positions is also wrong not to give thanks. He is, after all, not fettered with chains, nor attached by an iron to a post. Still, even the one in such circumstances has reason for thanksgiving: that he sees the sun, that he can breathe, that he can express thanks. Were you punished unjustly? Rejoice in hope for future good. Were you condemned rightly? So, too, thank God that you are paying for your offenses in this life and will not face eternal punishment for your sins. In these ways, the perceptive person can thank the benefactor throughout all conditions of life in proportion to present graces.

Most people scorn the present and demand what they lack. They do not consider the one who is more thirsty than they are as a cause for gratitude. Rather, they focus on the wide discrepancies between themselves and those above them, complaining about what others possess as if they have been robbed of what is their own. The slave is indignant at not being free. The free-born resents that he is not well-born of some aristocratic line, able to recite his ancestors back seven generations to some famous horse breeder, or to one who spent his wealth on the games. The aristocrat complains that he is not rich enough. The rich man is sad and resentful that he has no appointment that would give him power over cities and peoples. The military commander complains that he is not a king. And the king complains that he does not rule everything under the sun, that there are still some pockets of the earth not subject to his power. All of these fail to give their benefactor any thanks.

But let us not grieve over what we do not have. Let us learn to give thanks for the present. Let us mourn in right proportion, as the wise doctor says, *Your chastening was to us with small affliction*.[10] Let

[10]Is 26.16 (LXX).

us say, *It is good for me that you have afflicted me.*[11] We should say, *The sufferings of this present time are not worth comparing with the glory about to be revealed to us.*[12] We should say, *We are only scourged for a few of our sins.*[13] We should pray, *Chasten us, O Lord, but with judgment and not in anger.*[14] *For when we are judged by the Lord we are disciplined, so that we may not be condemned along with the world.*[15] In more fortunate circumstances will we speak the words of David, *What shall I return to the Lord for all his bounty to me?*[16] He has called us into being out of nothing; he has endowed us with reason, bestowed on us skills to help us preserve life; he has caused food to grow from the ground and has made the beasts subject to us. For our sake it rains, the sun shines, there are mountains and plains, and he has prepared for us places of shelter in the mountains even up to the highest peak. The rivers flow for our use, springs bubble up, the sea is open to us for trade, the mines for treasures. All that we enjoy, bestowed on us in all creation, we have around us through the rich and marvelous good of the creator.

7   But why limit examples to these small things? It was for our sake that God himself came to walk among humankind. For the sake of corruptible flesh the Word became flesh and lived among us. The creator tarried for the sake of ingrates; the sun of righteousness to those who sit in the shadows; the impassible went to the cross, life in death, light in the underworld, resurrection for the sake of those who had died, the adoption of the Holy Spirit, the promised allotment of God's grace, the promises of crowns. In short: everything beyond number, upon which fits the Prophet's utterance: *What shall I return to the Lord for all his bounty to me?*

[11]Ps 119.71 (118.71 LXX).
[12]Rom 8.18.
[13]Job 15.11.
[14]Jer 10.24.
[15]1 Cor 11.32.
[16]Ps 116.12 (115.3 LXX).

And these are not things our great Benefactor has simply given, but rather given back, as part of a grand cycle of giving. The thanks we render to him, he regards as so many good deeds, and holds us accountable. These assets that are given to you, advance them to the Benefactor by your alms through the hands of the poor, and although he has received his own property, so it is a perfect thanks, as if you have given from your own goods.[17] *What shall I return the Lord, for all his bounty to me?* I cannot let go of this saying of the Prophet, which sums up so well our present circumstance, as he sees his poverty and the deserving countergift of the Lord. Yet such magnanimous charity is nothing compared to the greater promises: the delights of paradise, the grandeur of heaven, angelic honor, the vision of God, the greatest good of all, honor, whatever each reasonable being desires, which portion we shall share after we put off the desires of the flesh.

How then shall we display to our neighbors this common sharing[18] and loving affection?[19] Ought we, when others are visited with terrible adversity, "weep" with them not by shedding tears but by giving thanks for their sorrow? It is true that it is a mark of patience and courage for each person to bear his particular sorrows in a spirit of thanksgiving. But only those who delight in others' afflictions will thank God for the misery of another, and such an attitude will aggravate their sorrow. Thus the Apostle tells us to *weep with those who weep.*[20] What should we say to this? Do I need to remind you of the Lord's saying about when one ought to rejoice and when one ought to mourn? *Rejoice*, he said, *and be glad, for your reward is great in heaven.*[21] And further on he says, *Daughters of Jerusalem, do not weep for me, but weep for your children.*[22] Therefore the Word tells us

---

[17]This concept of the gift cycle with its nuanced images of ownership, transfer, and reward, is a common theme in the Greek patristic texts that discuss philanthropy and divestment.

[18]Gk. τὸ κοινωνικόν.

[19]Gk. ἡ φιλοστοργία.

[20]Rom 12.15.

[21]Mt 5.12.

[22]Lk 23.28.

to rejoice and to exult with the righteous, but with those who repent, we should weep. We are to lament, indeed, to weep, over those who are lost, who lack right perception about their individual ruin.

8   But I don't believe that it fulfills the commandment if we weep and lament loudly with those bereaved by death. I would not think very highly of a physician who, instead of helping the sick, let himself fall victim to the same infection, or to a sea captain who, instead of commanding his sailors to labor against the wind, let the craft follow the waves, encouraging cowardice, became seasick, and lost courage along with the new recruits. It is the same with those who, in their sympathy with the bereaved, say nothing consoling but instead let themselves be carried away into the mourner's wild lamentations. You should suffer with the misfortune of those who mourn in such a way to prove to the other person that you are not rejoicing over their calamity nor indifferent to it. In this way you will make yourself their confidant and friend. But don't let yourself go over the edge, dragged down with them. Don't lament and mourn with them in a manner that imitates their behaviors, for example, by shutting yourselves up with them, dressing in black, sitting on the ground, or tearing out your hair. Such activities aggravate rather than alleviate their misfortune. Don't you see that when the swellings[23] and ailments of the spleen are traumatized, fever makes the pain worse, but a gentle touch of the hand has a soothing effect? Don't let your presence make the suffering worse, and do not fall with the one who has fallen. He who wants to lift up someone who is lying down must, after all, stand higher than that person; but if he himself falls, he will need another to pull him up. On the other hand, it is entirely appropriate to allow yourself to be moved by something that happens, and to mourn the misfortune in silence, in a dignified and serious manner, setting the tone for the occasion, engaging in conversation that does not blame or assign cause, like those do who mock the afflicted. Reproaches are a troublesome torture for those who are in sorrow; they are forced to

[23]Gk. βουβῶνες.

listen reluctantly to these heartless tirades and find them no comfort at all. But you should let mourning and lamentation be still, that the pain will soon pass, and then you may have opportunity to offer reasonable and gentle consolation.

Horse tamers do not tame wild colts by immediately pulling hard and steady on the reins of the bridle, nor do they use the spurs in the beginning. These methods would teach the horse to balk and throw off the rider. They start, instead, by pulling and then releasing, giving some slack to the reins. Only when they are beginning to become tame, their raging forces spent, then they accept the hard pull of the reins and learn obedience through the trainer's skill. It is, as Solomon said, *Better to come into a house of mourning than a house of pleasure*,[24] as long as one imparts there healing power through prudent and gentle consolation, not being infected by the sorrow as one might pick up a contagious eye disease.

9   So then, one must *weep with those who weep*. When you see your brother grieve, repent over his sins, weep with him and take part. Thus you can correct yourself through the others' sorrows. For the one who sheds hot tears over his neighbor's sins cures himself while lamenting for his brother. One such was he who said, *Despair seizes me because of the sinners who forsake your law*.[25] Mourn your own sins. Sin is the sickness of the soul, the death of what is immortal. It is right to weep and sigh over it. On sin's account tears ought to flow, sighs ought to continue, ascending upward out of the depths of the heart. Paul lamented the enemies of the cross of Christ.[26] Jeremiah mourned those among the people who had been slaughtered. Natural tears were not enough for him; he wanted them to become a spring of tears, and to go out into the desert, saying, *I will sit and mourn these people many days, who have been lost*.[27] This is the kind

---

[24]Eccl 7.3.
[25]Ps 119.53 (118.53 LXX).
[26]Phil 3.18.
[27]Jer 9.1.

of sorrow that glorifies the blessed Scriptures; not the tendency to burst out bawling at every opportunity.

I recently saw some pleasure lovers, people with an excessive thirst for delight, who abused mourning in this way, by making it an excuse for debauchery and drunkenness.[28] They sought to justify their behavior with Solomon's saying, *Give wine to those in distress.*[29] This is indeed the literal meaning, but it does not permit drunkenness, but rather is meant to help human life. The hidden meaning is not to think about sin, but rather "wine" refers to a reasonable joy. It does not mean that those who are disconsolate and dejected by excessive grief should neglect nourishment, but that the mourners should fortify their mind with bread, and use wine to strengthen what is weak. The wine-drinker and drunkard does not diminish grief by his behavior, but exchanges evil for evil, like merchants who cheat in the market, trading sickness of body for sickness of the soul, as if one might in the balance of scales weigh out so much sorrow on one side and on the other a proportionate increase in entertainment. I am of the opinion, however, that one can help nature by the use of wine, but not by pouring it down one's throat to the point of blinding all reason. The sorrow does not flow away with the wine, but indeed the soul is hardened to vice through such drunkenness. Insofar as reason is the best physician for grief, drunkenness is the greatest evil, impeding its cure.

So now, let each consider the teaching with your own reason, and you will appreciate the power of the apostolic command, and how it is both possible and useful: how you may indeed rejoice always, how you may pray without ceasing, how you may give thanks in all things. I think that you will see that this is indeed a consolation to the sorrowful, that through these words we may be made complete and perfect with the help of the Holy Spirit and the indwelling grace of our Lord Jesus Christ, to whom be glory and might, forever and ever. Amen.

[28]For more on Basil's view of drunkenness, see in this volume, Basil, *Homily Against Drunkards.*

[29]Prov 31.6.

On the Holy Martyr Mamas

1 I know all too well how important these festival sermons are. Indeed, it is precisely because I am not unaware of this that I feel quite inadequate to this task. The topic calls for something that the audience will consider worth their time, something that matches their hopes, both for the speaker and for the subject. And since we today commemorate the martyr with the greatest festivities, everyone is waiting with bated breath, attentive to hear something worthy of the martyr who has called us together.

Children who are raised properly will wish to give their fathers a fitting eulogy, and would be very displeased if a speaker's weakness compromises the great praise he deserves. The more you share this desire, the greater my risk. But what can I do? How can I satisfy your expectations so that you do not go home disappointed? I would suggest that each person, whatever memories he has brought with him of the martyr, call them to mind, that by sharing them together we might be refreshed with food for our journey home.

Remember the martyr. Let your minds dwell on how much he cheers you in your dreams; how, meeting you in this place he has helped you in your prayers; how much, when called on by name, he has assisted your work; accompanied you on your travels, helped in sickness; given back your children who were on the point of death; how he has lengthened lives! Let us collect these memories, creating an encomium from the shared portions. Together let each one share what he has with those who don't know anything about him. In this way those that lack may take in proportion to the gift, feasting on what you receive from one another, and, in this way, pardon our deficiency.

2   To praise the martyr is to dwell on his wealth in that spiritual gift of grace. For we cannot honor him as we might in the style of a worldly panegyric. He had no illustrious ancestor we can name. In addition, it would be unseemly to paint him with features suitable to those who are among the illustrious, for he stands with his own commendable virtue, although one usually uses such measures in describing a living person.[1] The law of truth, on the other hand, calls for praise suitable to each.

For it does not make a horse fast, that his sire won wealth at the racetrack. Neither does one praise a dog that is merely descended from a very fast racer. In the same way that we today judge animals according to whatever excellence they have individually, so too let us give each man praise according to the witness of his own right actions. How does a father's fame apply to his son? It is the same in the case of this martyr: he did not receive his fame from someone else, but is distinguished by the conduct of his own life, and this is what has ignited the torch of his glory. Mamas stands out from the rest; not others from Mamas. Children who have learned piety from him should praise him. He bubbled forth virtue. He does not boast falsely, as the waters from a fast-flowing mountain stream come from other tributaries further upstream; rather, out of his own vein flows his beauty.

Let us admire the man, not by adorning him with the beauty of others, but rather with his own illustrious qualities. Do you see famous horse breeders? Do you see their white sepulchers? How the past is reduced to a bare stone? But the memory of the martyr has drawn the whole countryside here today, with the entire city preparing for the feast. Not even family members are going to visit their ancestral graves, but all are hurrying to this place with its holy delight. This father of truth is our ancestral founder, although he is not named "father" according to the flesh. Do you see how people are

[1] That is, commemorating the dead focused on details such as family background and ancestors, while praise for the living (examples are most commonly political speeches that laud the emperor) was more likely to focus on personal characteristics and virtues (real or constructed).

honoring virtue and not riches? Thus it is that the Church honors the ones who have led us forward, as at the same time he exhorts us for the present life. Let us not aspire to wealth for ourselves, he says, neither to the unreliable wisdom of the world, nor to transitory glory. Such things disappear with this life. But be a holy laborer. For this is what you will take with you to heaven, leaving behind an immortal memory and acquiring permanent fame.

3   So then, if such is the memorial of a shepherd, let us not worship wealth. For we have gathered to praise one who had no wealth at all. Let us not go home marveling one who was rich, but one who had both poverty and piety.

A shepherd is no one of any significance. Nor does he practice any skilled craft. Wouldn't you be angry, even insulted, if someone provoked you by asking, "Are you a shepherd?" A shepherd possesses nothing beyond his daily food, a leather satchel, the staff he carries, and whatever he needs for that day, with no thought at all for the next. An enemy of wild beasts, associating with the tamest of all living creatures, he shuns the marketplace, flees from the law courts, knows nothing of social parasites,[2] nothing of trade, nothing of wealth; he does not have a roof over his head, living out under the open sky, at night gazing up to heaven and learning to know the creator from the wonder of the stars. A shepherd. Let us not be ashamed of the truth. Nor let us imitate the pagan myth-makers who embellish the truth with beautiful phrases. The truth is bare, without hired rhetoricians, defending itself by itself. To put it more bluntly: we have here a humble man, a poor shepherd, the pride of Christians. If our founding father is someone like this, a teacher of those who seek piety, well then, so were the fishermen and the tax collectors. So, too, were the disciples, some of them even leather-workers. No one was rich; no one was illustrious. All were of no account in worldly estimation. This is the kind of person we celebrate today, one we are delighted to honor, one we love so much that we alter our lives for

[2]That is, "sycophants" or slanderers.

his sake. And he is a shepherd, the one we venerate. So do not scorn such a leading figure.

You have heard that in the beginning Abel, who pleased God, was also a shepherd.[3] Who were his successors? Moses, the great lawgiver, who fled from Pharaoh's persecution when the hatred of his compatriots rose up against him, and became a shepherd on Mount Horeb, by which he became one who spoke with God. He was not perfecting the art of saying clever things in court when he saw the angel in the burning bush; he was out shepherding the flocks. And he was honored with a heavenly conversation. Who came after Moses? Jacob, the patriarch. He endured being a shepherd for the sake of the truth, this choice a witness to his whole character of life. To whom did he transmit this zeal? David. David came from shepherding the flocks when he was anointed king. The work of a shepherd and that of a king are comparable, with only a single difference: one is entrusted to oversee those that are irrational; the other those who are rational, and therefore the task requires greater knowledge. By joining both roles in himself, the Lord is both shepherd and king. He is shepherd over those who lack reason, and he brings those with reason under the mastery of his rule. Do you want to know how great a shepherd is? *The Lord is my shepherd.*[4] How is the king's post related to a shepherd's? *Who is the king of glory?*[5] The one who will be named the Great Shepherd is here called King.

And don't think that he himself was ashamed of this name; on the contrary. When he rebuffs the false shepherds, he uses this pastoral label for himself when he says, *I am the good shepherd.*[6] *I am* and *I do not change.*[7] And he says this bluntly, as when he speaks of his own greatness; for example, *I established the earth and I alone with my hand stretched out the heaven.*[8] And when the Word speaks of

[3] Gen 4.2. Scriptural citations follow the translation of the New Revised Standard Version unless noted otherwise (cf. *On Baptism*, note 1).

[4] Ps 23.1 (22.1 LXX).
[5] Ps 24.8 (23.8 LXX).
[6] Jn 10.11.
[7] Mal 3.6.
[8] Is 44.24.

all things worthy of God, he says, *I am the good shepherd*. He sends away the false shepherds and lays himself down as the truth. *I am the good shepherd*. Hear who is the good shepherd, and who is good! He explains it himself: *The true shepherd lays down his life for his sheep, but a hireling is not the shepherd, and the sheep do not hear him, nor does he care for them when he sees the wolf coming.*[9]

4   Here the Church[10] asks: If the Lord is the shepherd, then who is the hireling? Is it not the devil? And if the devil is the hireling, then who is the wolf? Surely the devil is a wolf: that wild, thieving, prowling beast, the common enemy of all. This is also the exact meaning of a hireling. The Lord says that false shepherds are those who have turned away. There are still such people in the present who deserve to be called hirelings, although they should not be. At the time when the Lord spoke, they were the high priest and the Pharisees, and all those of the sect of the Judaizers. He calls that one a hireling who is not of the truth, but also those who made a profit out of their appointed office as shepherds. These are the ones with whom "prayer" is a hollow pretense, who consume the bread that belongs to widows and orphans; thus they are hirelings. They serve their own advantage; they look only to care for the present and not the future; they are hirelings, not shepherds. Indeed today there are many hirelings, those who sell their life for a paltry portion of fame, and plot schism against the established doctrine of the Lord. They said this of the Lord, using him to create schism. For one said, *He has a demon*,[11] and another said, *A demon cannot give sight to the one who was born blind*.[12] Do you see how far back this tendency runs to schism? For it says that the winnowing fork will divide the straw from the wheat;[13] and that which is lightweight and volatile will be separated out from

---

[9]Jn 10.11–12.

[10]Gk. ἡ ἐκκλησία. Here Basil leads the audience toward his warning against the false teachers who upset and divide the church with divergent views about the nature and divinity of the Son.

[11]Jn 8.48.

[12]Jn 9.16.

[13]Lk 3.17.

what can truly provide nourishment, that is, what is serviceable as spiritual nourishment, that is what the farmer will keep as his own. By this division, some will be placed in one place, others in another place. It is fitting for the Jews to create schism, but the church of God should be like that seamless garment, woven above and below, the coat that Christ had worn, which the soldiers took and did not tear. *And I know my own and my own know me.*[14] These words the heretics twist and tear apart, to corroborate with their blasphemies. "Look," they say, "My own know me and I know my own."

What is that which is known? Is it to understand the measure of greatness? Who is brazen enough to claim that he can comprehend divinity? Or do you not see from what follows, that it concerns a certain understanding? What do we understand of God in the words, *My sheep hear my voice*? Do you see how God can be perceived? In that, namely, we hear his commands, and that we hear and obey them. In this is the knowledge of God, that we observe God's command. It is not in long investigation over God's essence; not in examining the supernatural; not in brooding over things that are invisible. "My own know me and I know my own." It is enough for you to know that he is a good shepherd, that he has given his life[15] for the sheep. That is the limit of knowing God. How great God is, his measurable dimensions, in what his essence consists—to ask such things is perilous and impossible to answer. On these points it is best to remain silent. *My sheep hear my voice.* They hear, he says, but not "They brood over." They are not disobedient, not quarrelsome.

Having heard "Son," do not quibble with me about manners of begetting; do not dream up an explanation for what is inexplicable; do not by schism divide what is a conjunction. Therefore the evangelist tells you from the start what you can know with certainty. You have heard it before; hear it now again: *In the beginning was the Word.*[16] From this you do not conclude the Son to have had a

---

[14]Jn 10.14.
[15]Gk. ψυχή.
[16]Jn 1.1.

normal birth, that he is one who had not previously existed. *Word*, he says, to explain that he is impassible; *was*, he says to you to note the absence of time;[17] *beginning*, he says to you to teach you that he was in coexistent contact with the Father. *In the beginning* plus *was* plus *the Word*.

Do not say, "How was it?" and "If it was, then he was not engendered," and "If he was engendered, then there was a time when he did not exist." The one who says things like this does not belong to the flock. He is a wolf disguised as a sheep. Recognize such deceit for what it is. *My sheep hear my voice*. Have you heard "Son"? Know that he is like the Father; a "likeness,"[18] I say, on account of the weakness of the powers of the body. Indeed, this is the truth (do not be afraid to accept the truth); I am not one disposed to slander. They are identical,[19] I say; while maintaining the distinction of Father and Son.[20] In the hypostasis of the Son, understand the form of the Father, in order that you may preserve exactly what it means for the Son to be the image of God, so that you will know from it the way of true piety, and what it means, that *I am in the Father and the Father in me*.[21] Do not think this is some mixture of essences; rather, they are identical in character.[22]

So then, beloved, we have here the greatest contradiction: that our weakness might bring out your good pleasure at hearing what I have to say, in order that the power of God might be manifest with an enlightenment that comes from such a debilitated instrument as I am. Perhaps so truly great was my weakness that the one we gather today to commemorate has been that much more glorified, strengthened in weakness! May the assembly of our festival, as we come to the end of the prayers of last year and begin again (for this day is at the end of the circle of the past year, and the beginning of

[17]Gk. τὸ ἄχρονον.
[18]Gk. ὁμοιότητα.
[19]Gk. ταυτότητα.
[20]Gk. φυλάσσων Υἱοῦ καὶ Πατρὸς ἰδιότητα.
[21]Jn 14.10.
[22]Gk. οὐκ οὐσιῶν σύγχυσιν ἀλλὰ χαρακτήρων ταυτότητα.

next),[23] according to the grace and strength of intentions for our future gatherings, be closely guarded with the powerful defense of the martyr, preserved from all disturbances and attacks of heresy. And in peace may he enable us to learn the divine Word and be supplied with the grace of the Spirit. To Him be glory and power together with the Holy Spirit, now and always, and into eternity of eternities.[24] Amen.

[23]Basil's comment here places the sermon at the start of the new year in the calendar followed in Caesarea in Cappadocia in the mid fourth-century, possibly early October (see Introduction).

[24]Gk. νῦν καὶ ἀεί, καὶ εἰς τοὺς αἰῶνας τῶν αἰώνων.

On the Martyr Barlaam

1   In former times, they used to honor the death of saints with lamentations and tears. Joseph wept aloud when he heard that Jacob was dead;[1] the Jews mourned deeply the death of Moses;[2] and honored Samuel with much weeping.[3] But in these days we celebrate the death of the holy ones with a festival. For the nature of grief has been reversed by the cross. No longer do we keep watch at the death of saints with dirges, but dance victoriously with inspired choruses at their tombs.

For death is sleep to the righteous. More than sleep, it is a departure to a better life. This is why the martyrs leap with joy when they are slaughtered. For the yearning for the blessed life kills the death-pain of the slaughter. The martyr does not see danger, but victory crowns. He does not shudder at the blows, but calculates what will follow, with no eye down to the public executioner's blows but rather to the angels sounding triumphantly on high. He does not think about passing dangers but eternal reward. And even now among us, they reap a foretaste of that [heavenly] promise, as they receive reverent applause from all, their tombs, like nets, drawing in the pilgrim crowds.

2   This is what is taking place at the tomb of the noble Barlaam. For the martyr's battle trumpet has sounded, and you see the soldiers of praise gather. The presentation is announced, the athlete of Christ stretched out here, and the vehement excitement of the church is like a theater. And as the Lord of the faithful says, *Those who believe in*

[1] Gen 50.1.
[2] Deut 34.2.
[3] 1 Sam 25.1.

me, even though they die, will live.[4] Although the noble Barlaam has been taken, he organizes the festivities;[5] consumed by the grave, he invites [us] to a feast.

Now is the appointed time for us to shout aloud, *Where is the one who is wise? Where is the scribe? Where is the debater of this age?*[6] Today a country bumpkin is our unconquered teacher of piety. He whom the tyrant caught in the net like easy prey was seen, after the trial, to be in truth an unconquered soldier; he derided him on account of his broken accent, but trembled at his angelic energies.[7] For his way of life was not barbaric like his speech, his reason sound without the defects in his syllables; rather, he imitated Paul, who said, *I may be untrained in speech, but not in knowledge.*[8]

The public executioners were exhausted from flogging him, but the martyr proved stronger than they, wearying the hands[9] of those lacerating him, but the determination of the one being beaten did not bend. Even when the whips tore apart the harmony of his musculature, the lashings bound up his faith to its consummate perfection.[10] His lacerated ribs were spent, but the self-discipline of his mind flourished. His body had been deadened, but his strength was as if he had not yet begun the battle. For whenever love of piety has prepared the soul, any type of attack seems absurd, and all the shredding of his flesh for the sake of that for which he longed was for him, more like entertainment than torture. This reminds me of the apostles' desire, who rejoiced when they were beaten by the Jews: *As they left the council*, it says, *they rejoiced that they suffered dishonor for the sake of the name.*[11]

---

[4] Jn 11.25.

[5] Gk. πανήγυρις.

[6] 1 Cor 1.20.

[7] Gk. νεανιευόμενον, lit. "youthful bravado."

[8] 2 Cor 11.6.

[9] Gk. αἱ χεῖρες, which may also mean "arms," though here more likely a deliberate comparison with the saint's strong hand.

[10] Note here the metaphorical image: the body's literal tearing apart of muscles/sinews creates a unifying effect on the substance of faith.

[11] Acts 5.41.

Such also was this soldier we praise today: He regarded his torture as a reason for good cheer; the floggings felt to him like a gentle pelting with roses, the temper of the judge like a wisp of smoke. He derided the savage regiment of soldiers, dancing in the chorus of dangers as if they were crowns. He was cheered by the blows as if being honored, exulting in the most violent tortures as if rewarded with some eminence. He spits on the naked swords. He regarded the hands of the public executioners as softer than wax, embracing the wooden block of his torture like salvation. He delighted in the bindings of those shackling him as if they were the charms of a verdant meadow, enjoying the designs of tortures as if they were multicolored blossoms. He kept his right hand more vigorous than the fire. Indeed, this was the enemy's final torturous machination against him.

For they lit up an altar for libations to the demons and brought the martyr to stand beside it. They ordered that he hold his right hand, palm up, suspending it over the altar, perversely using the hand as if it were a bronze sacrificial bowl, villainously placing smoldering incense in it. For they hoped that the fire's heat might master the hand, forcing the incense to drop onto the altar. Alas, such are the entangled connivances of the ungodly! Then, since countless tortures had failed to result in the desired effect, the strife-loving adversary sought to force submission by fire to his hand, saying, "Since we have not shaken his soul with subtle tricks, let us at least jar his right hand by applying it to the fire." But again their hope was dashed. For although the flame gnawed through the hand, he held the flame in his hand as if it were ash. The fire did not turn it around, as cowards in war turn their backs, but he stood unmoved, besting the flame. The martyr admonished them with the words of the Prophet, *Blessed be the Lord, my God, who trains my hands for battle*.[12] For he stretched out his hand in the fire, and the fire was defeated. The flame and the right hand of the martyr wrestled together in battle, but the unexpected victor of the wrestling bout

[12]Ps 144.1 (143.1 LXX).

was the right hand, the hand encircling the flame, yet fully extended
for battle. O hand, more battle-eager than fire! O hand, that did not
submit to the sensation of the fire! O fire, defeated by the instruction
of the hand! Iron is subject to the power of fire, which makes it soft.
Bronze, too, yields to the mastery of fire; it conquers even the force
of stone. But, despite the overpowering force of the flame, it did not
bend the martyr's outstretched right hand, although burning it out.

3   Reasonably, then, might the martyr cry out, saying of the Lord,
*You hold my right hand. You guide me with your counsel, and after-
ward you will receive me with honor.*[13] What will I call you, O noble
soldier of Christ? Shall I call you a statue? That would deeply dispar-
age your patient endurance. For fire can soften whatever receives it;
but it could not cause your right hand to be visibly moved at all. If
I were to call you iron, this image, too, falls short of your valor. For
you alone convinced the flames not to overpower your hand. Your
right hand alone exposed the place of sacrifice; your right hand,
alone, aflame, slapped the demons in the face, the roasting hand
melting their heads. It blinded them with its ashes, trampling them
under foot.

    But why do I diminish this memorial like a child who does not
pronounce words clearly? Let us now give way to the tongues of
those whose offer the martyr hymns of far greater magnificence; let
us call on the lofty trumpeting calls of the teachers.[14] Rise up now,
you painters whose colors radiate with the glow suitable to a champion; use your skills to improve this imperfect image of our leader.
What my sketch has obscured of his crowning, show his colors by

[13] Ps 73.23b–24 (72.24 LXX).

[14] Pauline Allen suggests that the rich iconographic allusions here, to the creation
of other vivid imagery, refers in fact to other speakers who, as part of the festival, were
waiting in the assembly to follow this sermon with their own praise of the martyr. Pauline Allen, "Loquacious Locals: Two Indigenous Martyrs in the Homilies of Severus of
Antioch," in J. Leemans, ed. *Martyrdom and Persecution in Late Antique Christianity:
Festschrift Boudewijn Dehandschutter*, Bibliotheca Ephemeridum Theologicarum
Lovaniensium 241 (Leuven: Peeters, 2010), 1–14, at 13.

your artistic design. I wish to concede, vanquished by your winning power. Let me rejoice in your clear depictions of the battle, envisioning the hand toward the fire. Let me see your brightest illustration of the image of the wrestler. Let the demons wail, and be smitten by your representation of the martyr's prowess. Show them again the burning hand exhibiting its victory. Let it be inscribed on a painted tablet,[15] and also Christ, who presides over the combat, to whom be the glory unto eternity of eternities. Amen.

---

[15]Gk. ἐγγραφέσθω τῷ πίνακι.

Select Bibliography

Texts and Translations

Basil of Caesarea. "Protreptic on Holy Baptism," Thomas Halton, trans. In *Baptism: Ancient Liturgies and Patristic Texts*, 75–87. Edited by André Hamman. Staten Island, NY: Alba House, 1967.

Deferrari, Roy J., trans. *St. Basil: The Letters*. Loeb Classical Library. Cambridge, MA: Harvard University Press, 4 vols. 1926–1934.

DelCogliano, Mark. *St. Basil the Great: On Christian Doctrine and Practice*. Popular Patristics Series 47. Yonkers, NY: St Vladimir's Seminary Press, 2012.

DelCogliano, Mark and Andrew Radde-Gallwitz. *Basil of Caesarea: Against Eunomius*. Fathers of the Church 122. Washington, DC: Catholic University of America Press, 2011.

De Sinner, Gabriel Rudolf Ludwig. *Sancti Patris nostri Basilii, Caesareae Cappadociae archiepiscopi, opera omnia quae exstant, vel quae sub eius nomine circumferuntur, ad manuscriptos Codices Gallicanos, Vaticanos, Florentinos et Anglicos, necnon ad antiquiores editiones castigata, multis aucta: Nova Interpretatione, criticis Praefationibus, Notis, variis Lectionibus illustrata, nova sancti Doctoris Vita et copioissimis Indicibus locupletata. Tomus Primus et Secundus: Opera et studio Domni Iuliani Garnier, Presbyteri et Monachi Benedictini, e Congregatione Sancti Mauri. Tomus Tertius: Opera et studio Monachorum Ordinis Sancti Benedicti, et Congregatione Sancti Mauri*. Editio Parisina altera, emendata et aucta. Paris: Gaume Fratres, 1839.

Garnier, Julien, and Prudentius Maran. *Sancti Patris nostri Basilii, Caesareae Cappadociae archiepiscopi, opera omnia quae exstant, vel quae sub eius nomine circumferuntur, ad manuscriptos Codices Gallicanos, Vaticanos, Florentinos et Anglicos, necnon ad antiquiores editiones castigata, multis aucta: Nova Interpretatione, criticis Praefationibus, Notis, variis Lectionibus illustrata, nova sancti Doctoris Vita et copioissimis Indicibus locupletata. Tomus Primus et Secundus: Opera et studio Domni Iuliani Garnier, Presbyteri et Monachi Benedictini, e Congregatione Sancti Mauri. Tomus Tertius: Opera et studio Monachorum Ordinis Sancti Benedicti, et Congregatione Sancti Mauri.* Paris: Coigard, 1721–1730.

Harrison, Nonna Verna, trans. *St Basil the Great: On the Human Condition.* Popular Patristics Series 30. Crestwood, NY: St Vladimir's Seminary Press, 2005.

Hildebrand, Stephen, trans. *Basil of Caesarea: On the Holy Spirit.* Popular Patristics Series 42. Yonkers, NY: St Vladimir's Seminary Press, 2011.

Jackson, Blomfield, "The Treatise *de Spiritu Sancto,* the Nine Homilies of the *Hexaemeron* and the *Letters.*" Nicene and Post-Nicene Fathers [NPNF], series 2, vol. 8. Edinburgh: T & T Clark, 1894, repr. Grand Rapids: Wm. B. Eerdmans, 1989.

Kendrick, Francis Patrick, trans. *A Treatise on Baptism, with an Exhortation to Receive it, Translated from the Works of St. Basil the Great, To which is added a Treatise on Confirmation.* Philadelphia: M. Fithian, 1843.

Lewis, George, trans. *The Philocalia of Origen: A Compilation of Selected Passages from Origen's Works made by St. Gregory of Nazianzus and St. Basil of Caesarea.* Edinburgh: T & T clark, 1911; online at: <http://www.tertullian.org/fathers/origen_philocalia_01_intro.htm.>

Lipatov, Nikolai A., trans. *St. Basil the Great: Commentary on the Prophet Isaiah.* Texts and Studies in the History of Theology 7. Mandelbachtal/Cambridge: edition cicero, 2001.

Mayer, Wendy, with Bronwen Neil (trans). *St John Chrysostom: The Cult of the Saints: Select Homilies and Letters.* Popular Patristics Series 31. Crestwood, NY: St Vladimir's Seminary Press, 2006.

Schroeder, C. Paul, trans. *St Basil the Great: On Social Justice.* Popular Patristics Series 38. Crestwood, NY: St Vladimir's Seminary Press, 2009.

Severus of Antioch, Homily 73 "Sur le saint martyr Barlaha," *Patrologia Orientalis* 12.2 (1919): 90–96. Edited and translated by Maurice Brière.

Silvas, Anna M., trans. *The Asketikon of St Basil the Great.* Oxford Early Christian Studies. Oxford: Oxford University Press, 2005.

Wagner, Sister M. Monica, trans. *Saint Basil: Ascetical Works.* The Fathers of the Church 9. New York: Fathers of the Church, 1950.

Way, Agnes Clare, trans. *Saint Basil: Exegetic Homilies.* The Fathers of the Church 46. Washington, DC: Catholic University of America Press, 1963.

_____. *Saint Basil: Letters. Volume 1 (1–185)*. Fathers of the Church 13. New York: The Fathers of the Church, Inc., 1951.

_____. *Saint Basil: Letters. Volume 2 (186–368)*. Fathers of the Church 28. New York: The Fathers of the Church, Inc., 1955.

Studies

Allen, Pauline. "Loquacious Locals: Two Indigenous Martyrs in the Homilies of Severus of Antioch." In *Martyrdom and Persecution in Late Antique Christianity: Festschrift Boudewijn Dehandschutter*, 1–14. Edited by Johan Leemans. Bibliotheca Ephemeridum Theologicarum Lovaniensium 241. Leuven: Peeters, 2010.

Beagon, Philip M. "The Cappadocian Fathers, Women and Ecclesiastical Politics." *Vigiliae Christianae* 49.2 (May 1995): 165–79.

Bernardi, Jean. *La prédication des Pères Cappadociens: Le prédicateur et son auditoire*. Publications de la faculté des lettres et sciences humaines de l'Université de Montpellier 30. Montpellier: Presses Universitaires de France, 1968.

DelCogliano, Mark. "Tradition and Polemic in Basil of Caesarea's Homily on the Theophany." *Vigiliae Christianae* 65 (2011): 30–55.

Delehaye, Hippolyte. *Les origines du culte des martyrs*. Subsidia Hagiographica 20. Brussels: Société des Bollandistes, 1933.

_____. "S. Barlaam: Martyr à Antioche." *Analecta Bollandiana* 22 (1903): 129–45.

Driver, Lisa D. Maugans. "The Cult of Martyrs in Asterius of Amaseia's Vision of the Christian City." *Church History* 74.2 (June 2005): 236–54.

Esteves Pereira, Francisco Maria. *O santo martyr Barlaam: Estudo de critica historica*. Coimbra [Portugal]: Imprensa de universidade, 1901.

Fedwick, Paul Jonathan, ed. *Basil of Caesarea: Christian, Humanist, Ascetic. A Sixteenth-Hundredth Anniversary Symposium*. 2 vols. Toronto: The Pontifical Institute of Mediaeval Studies, 1981.

_____. *Bibliotheca Basiliana Vniversalis*. 5 vols. Turnhout: Brepols, 1993–2005.

Gemeinhardt, Peter, and Johan Leemans, eds. *Christian Martyrdom in Late Antiquity (300–450 AD): History, Discourse, Tradition and Religious Identity*. Berlin: DeGruyter, 2012.

Harrison, Verna E.F. "Male and Female in Cappadocian Theology." *Journal of Theological Studies* NS 42, part 2 (October 1990): 441–71.

Havryliv, Rev. Fr. Matey, OSBM. "Prayer in Life and Works of Saint Basil."
    Blogpost of the Commission on Basilian Monasticism, Posted June 13,
    2012 at: <http://osbmcommission.wordpress.com/list-of-conferences/
    on-prayer-in-the-teaching-rule-and-life-of-st-basil/>.

Hildebrand, Stephen M. *The Trinitarian Theology of Basil of Caesarea: A Syn-
    thesis of Greek Thought and Biblical Truth*. Washington, DC: Catholic
    University of America Press, 2007.

Holman, Susan R. *The Hungry are Dying: Beggars and Bishops in Roman
    Cappadocia*. Oxford Studies in Historical Theology. New York: Oxford
    University Press, 2001.

Leemans, Johan. "Celebrating the Martyrs: Early Christian Liturgy and the
    Martyr Cult in Fourth Century Cappadocia and Pontus." *Questions
    Liturgiques/Studies in Liturgy* 82 (2001): 247–67.

———. "Martyr, Monk and Victor of Paganism: An Analysis of Basil of
    Caesarea's Panegyrical Sermon on Gordius." In *More Than A Memory:
    The Discourse of Martyrdom and the Construction of Christian Identity
    in the History of Christianity*, 45–78. Edited by Johan Leemans. Annua
    Nuntia Lovaniensia 51. Leuven: Peeters, 2005.

———. "Preaching Christian Virtue: Basil of Caesarea's Panegyrical Ser-
    mon on Julitta." In *Virtutis Imago: Studies on the Conceptualisation and
    Transformation of an Ancient Ideal*, 259–84. Edited by Gert Partoens,
    Geert Roskam, and Toon Van Houdt. Leuven: Peeters, 2004.

Limberis, Vasiliki. "The Cult of the Martyrs and the Cappadocian Fathers."
    In *Byzantine Christianity*, 39–48. Edited by Derek Kruger. A People's
    History of Christianity 3. Minneapolis: Augsburg Fortress, 2010.

Limberis, Vasiliki. *Architects of Piety: The Cappadocian Fathers and the Cult
    of the Martyrs*. New York: Oxford University Press, 2011.

Marti, H. "Rufinus' Translation of St. Basil's Sermon on Fasting." *Studia
    Patristica* 16 (1985): 418–22.

Marti, Heinrich. *Rufin von Aquileia: De Ieiunio I, II: Zwei Predigten über das
    Fasten nach Basileios von Kaisareia*. Vigiliae Christianae Supplements
    6. Leiden: Brill, 1989.

Métivier, Sophie. *La Cappadoce (IVe-Vie siècle): Une histoire provinciale de
    l'Empire romain d'Orient*. Byzantina Sorbonensia 22. Paris: Publications
    de la Sorbonne, 2005.

Radde-Gallwitz, Andrew. *Basil of Caesarea: A Guide to his Life and Doctrine*.
    Eugene, OR: Cascade Books, 2012.

Rousseau, Philip. *Basil of Caesarea*. Berkeley: University of California Press, 1994.

Skedros, James C. "The Cappadocian Fathers on the Veneration of Martyrs." *Studia Patristica* 37 (1999): 294–300. Published by Leuven: Peeters, 2001.

————. "Shrines, Festivals, and the 'Undistinguished Mob,'" In *Byzantine Christianity*, 81–102. Edited by Derek A. Krueger. A People's History of Christianity 3. Minneapolis: Augsburg Fortress, 2010.

————. "The Greek Fathers on the Lives of the Saints: Towards a Hermeneutic of Hagiography." Unpublished discussion paper for Patristica Bostoniensia. December 18, 2003.

Smith, Richard Travers. *St. Basil the Great*. The Fathers for English Readers. London: Society for Promoting Christian Knowledge, 1879.

Van Dam, Raymond. *Kingdom of Snow: Roman Rule and Greek Culture in Cappadocia*. Philadelphia: University of Pennsylvania Press, 2002.

————. *Becoming Christian: The Conversion of Roman Cappadocia*. Philadelphia: University of Pennsylvania Press, 2003.

————. *Families and Friends in Late Roman Cappadocia*. Philadelphia: University of Pennsylvania Press, 2003.

POPULAR PATRISTICS SERIES

ST VLADIMIR'S SEMINARY PRESS
1-800-204-2665 • www.svspress.com